Praise for **THE PO****RE**

"In a noisy world where high ⬚⬚⬚⬚⬚⬚⬚⬚⬚⬚⬚⬚⬚⬚⬚⬚⬚⬚ to discover Dane Jensen. *The Pow*⬚⬚⬚⬚⬚⬚⬚⬚⬚⬚⬚⬚⬚⬚*ng*, and
practical. You'll learn how to nail the moments that matter—and you'll
also manage pressure to your benefit over the long term. Both skillsets
are required of enduring leaders. Once you become a standout, you can
teach Dane's 'pressure management' to your people and gain an unassail-
able advantage for your organization."

> —**DORIE CLARK**, adjunct professor at Duke University's Fuqua School
> of Business, executive education faculty, and author of *Stand Out*

"Imagine what you could accomplish if you could disarm your biggest
pressures—then put their energy to work. Dane Jensen shows how in
this timely book. Relentless pressures are here to stay. Get fresh advice
from *The Power of Pressure*, for the next crisis or for your long-term
performance."

> —**AMY EDMONDSON**, Novartis professor of leadership
> and management at Harvard Business School

"I wish I could have read this when I was starting out. Dane Jensen has created an invaluable formula for understanding pressure and using it to drive
innovation and overcome challenges. *The Power of Pressure* is an invaluable
field guide to the age of pressure for the next generation of global leaders."

> —**DR. KEVIN FREY**, CEO, Generation Unlimited

"Entertaining and insightful! Dane Jensen has disproven the notion that
the only thing to be done about pressure is to cope with it. *The Power of
Pressure* demonstrates how pressure can be transformed into growth. It
lays out an easy-to-follow framework that is helpful to experienced and
emerging leaders alike. A great resource for anyone who wants to excel
under pressure."

> —**STEVEN GOLDBACH**, chief strategy officer, Deloitte

"Insightful! *The Power of Pressure* will teach you to watch for the patterns and traps that hold you back from achieving your highest potential. Dane Jensen has provided the keys to lowering stress and freeing yourself to enjoy life!"

—MARSHALL GOLDSMITH, #1 *New York Times* bestselling author
of *Triggers, Mojo,* and *What Got You Here Won't Get You There*

"Dane Jensen has already provided great help, wisdom, and insight to me and our staff at Canada Basketball—from working on our strategic planning to resilience training. Now, *The Power of Pressure* provides all of us with key learnings, strategies, and techniques to deal with the pressures we all face. Dane's guidance can help make us more resilient, happier, and productive."

—GLEN GRUNWALD, former general manager of the Toronto Raptors
and the New York Knicks

"Dane Jensen's book drills down to how we act when the heat's on high—because how we manage our peak-pressure moments makes all the difference. Dane's reader-friendly framework keeps everything simple. His research is fresh. And his inspiring stories help put best-in-class outcomes within reach again and again. No doubt, *The Power of Pressure* will be a game-changer for so many."

—MATT HIGGINS, chairman and CEO, Omnichannel Acquisition
Corp., and co-founder and CEO, RSE Ventures

"A leader's quest for impact begins inside. That's why I'm fired up about *The Power of Pressure*. Dane Jensen uses personal stories, brain/body research, and pressure-treated advice to demonstrate how to manage all kinds of forces to your benefit. The book is a remarkably useful guide for anyone looking to transform their leadership practice."

—ALDEN MILLS, Inc. 500 CEO, Navy SEAL,
and author of *Unstoppable Teams*

"I've studied leadership for years, and I can tell you Dane Jensen's *The Power of Pressure* is pure leadership alchemy. Dane is one of the first thought leaders to truly elaborate on the full value of pressure. He shares conversations with some of our most remarkable leaders about how pressure enhances their performance, and that's gold in our pressure-packed world. Dane also shows us how to handle pressure the right way—not only to drive results but to improve the lives of those we lead. *The Power of Pressure* is a must-read for what we are likely going to call 'our new decade of pressure.'"

—THOMAS A. KOLDITZ, PhD; brigadier general, USA (ret.); professor emeritus, West Point; founding director of Doerr Institute for New Leaders at Rice University; and author of *In Extremis Leadership* and *Leadership Reckoning*

"This is the best book I've read on pressure and performance. If you want to win a championship, it's not enough to just handle pressure. You need to use pressure to get better every day. *The Power of Pressure* lays out a clear set of tactics to help you use pressure as an advantage. If you're on the lookout for practical ways to up your game when it matters most—read this book."

—NICK NURSE, former head coach of the NBA championship-winning Toronto Raptors

"A phenomenal read! *The Power of Pressure* is a truly unique view of what it takes to rise to the demands life places upon us. Dane Jensen has taken the bold stance that pressure is something that can be enjoyed. He's backed it up with compelling research and brought it to life through vivid and fascinating storytelling. I can't wait to see what the next generation of Olympians will achieve with this book in their arsenal."

—DAVID SHOEMAKER, CEO and secretary general, Canadian Olympic Committee

"Dane Jensen has been a tremendous partner in helping us develop our leaders at the USGA. Filled with stories of pressure—from sports to the military, to work and home life—*The Power of Pressure* is an excellent read. The book radiates with practical advice for achieving meaningful and sustained results as a leader, volunteer, or competitor."

—**STEVE SCHLOSS**, chief people officer, USGA

"Grounded in data, Dane Jensen has an incredibly clear view of the world and how people strive and thrive in the face of daunting circumstances. Dane provides razor-sharp insight with practical advice that is clear and easy to digest. A must-read to take you and your team to the next level."

—**KAREN O'NEILL**, CEO, Canadian Paralympic Committee

"*The Power of Pressure* is a brilliant read that captures the essence of pressure and offers expert advice for using it to fuel performance. Read this book. It will make you better at nailing the moments that matter, and for navigating a high-pressure life over the long haul."

—**DR. HAYLEY WICKENHEISER**, OC,
four-time Olympic gold medalist and Hockey Hall of Fame inductee

"This book comes at the perfect time! Our clients' demand for skills to navigate pressure has never been higher—and *The Power of Pressure* has answered their call. Dane Jensen turns stress management on its head and transforms pressure from something to endure into something that drives you."

—**DAVE ROBERTS**, president, UNC Executive Development

"*The Power of Pressure* is grounded in research, full of useful tools, and packed full of riveting stories that bring the concepts to life. Dane Jensen's approach to pressure has benefited thousands of our students and his wisdom shines through here."

—**ELSPETH MURRAY**, associate dean of MBA and masters programs at
the Smith School of Business at Queen's University

"If higher performance and personal growth matter to you, this is your roadmap. In *The Power of Pressure*, Dane Jensen lays out three forces that can set you up for your personal best. He shows how we can capitalize on pressure's pure energy. It will help to lead you and others forward to a better life. Unleash the Power of Pressure in your life!"

—**CHESTER ELTON**, bestselling author of
The Carrot Principle, All In, and *Anxiety at Work*

"Dane Jensen's easy-to-grasp framework shows how to convert the powers of pressure from detriments into assets that enhance performance in all parts of life. His advice is fresh and his terrific storytelling sheds new light on how to cope with the demands of our pressure-packed world. Read *The Power of Pressure* to help you lead with greater success and less stress."

—**STEW FRIEDMAN**, The Wharton School,
bestselling author of *Total Leadership*

"Dane put a lot of pressure on me to write this testimonial. Fortunately, I use the techniques taught in this wonderful book and handle pressure well. So here's the damn testimonial."

—**DAVID CHILTON**, bestselling author of
The Wealthy Barber and former dragon on *Dragons' Den*

"The most effective crisis leaders I work with through Harvard's National Preparedness Leadership Initiative have learned to thrive under pressure. In *The Power of Pressure*, Dane Jensen explains why. It is a matter of understanding yourself and how to shape your relationship with pressure in order to reap its benefits without succumbing to its traps. Through inspiring stories and approachable interpretations of psychology and neuroscience, Jensen explains how to use pressure to foster high performance without burning yourself—and others—out. This is essential reading for those called upon to lead when everything is on the line."

—**ERIC J. MCNULTY**, crisis leadership expert and co-author of
You're It: Crisis, Change, and How to Lead When It Matters Most

"*The Power of Pressure* is a smart look at how it wields its power over us, but also how it unleashes our potential. This timely book—shows how you can set yourself up to be your most productive, most successful, and also least stressed self by turning the pressure you feel into an advantage."

—DAVID BURKUS, Thinkers50 ranked thought leader and bestselling author of *Leading from Anywhere*

THE
POWER
OF
PRESSURE

WHY PRESSURE ISN'T THE PROBLEM,
IT'S THE SOLUTION

DANE JENSEN

Collins

Published by Collins, an imprint of HarperCollins Publishers Ltd

First published by Collins in a hardcover edition: 2021
This trade paperback edition: 2023

Illustrations by James Jensen/Atom Studio.

HarperCollins books may be purchased for educational, business, or sales
promotional use through our Special Markets Department.

HarperCollins Publishers Ltd
Bay Adelaide Centre, East Tower
22 Adelaide Street West, 41st Floor
Toronto, Ontario, Canada
M5H 4E3

www.harpercollins.ca

Library and Archives Canada Cataloguing in Publication

Title: The power of pressure : why pressure isn't the problem, it's the solution / Dane Jensen.
Names: Jensen, Dane, author.
Description: Includes bibliographical references and index.
Identifiers: Canadiana 20220467420 | ISBN 9781443461573 (softcover)
Subjects: LCSH: Stress (Psychology) | LCSH: Stress (Physiology) | LCSH: Stress management. |
LCSH: Success—Psychological aspects.
Classification: LCC BF575.S75 J46 2023 | DDC 155.9/042—dc23

Printed and bound in the United States of America
23 24 25 26 27 LBC 5 4 3 2 1

FOR MY PARENTS,
PETER AND SANDRA

CONTENTS

1   **INTRODUCTION** No Pressure, No Diamonds

PART 1
UNDERSTANDING PRESSURE

9   **CHAPTER 1** The Pressure Equation: The Interplay of
Importance, Uncertainty, and Volume

25   **CHAPTER 2** Blood, Sweat, and Breath: How Your Body
Handles Pressure

47   **CHAPTER 3** Becoming Pressure Ambidextrous:
Performance in the Moment and Over Time

PART 2
HARNESSING THE POWER OF PRESSURE

67   **CHAPTER 4** Connect with Why It Matters: Importance
Over the Long Haul

93   **CHAPTER 5** See What's *Not* at Stake: Importance in Peak
Pressure Moments

115 **CHAPTER 6** Take Direct Action: Uncertainty in Peak
Pressure Moments

139 **CHAPTER 7** Embrace Inevitable Uncertainty: Uncertainty
Over the Long Haul

165 **CHAPTER 8** Simplify: Volume in Peak Pressure Moments

183 **CHAPTER 9** Sleep and Other Inconvenient Necessities:
Volume Over the Long Haul

PART 3
PUTTING IT ALL TOGETHER

219 **CHAPTER 10** The Limits of Independence: Recruiting Support That Works

237 **CHAPTER 11** Pressure, Attention, and Preparation: Using the Pressure Canvas

261 **ACKNOWLEDGMENTS**

265 **SOURCES**

281 **INDEX**

INTRODUCTION

NO PRESSURE, NO DIAMONDS

Every summer, my wife, our three kids—Jack, Stella, and Henry—and I spend as much time as we can at our cottage north of Toronto. We are lucky enough to have a family compound, with my family, my parents, and my sister's family all having cabins side by side.

One day at the cottage, my wife went out for a run, leaving Grandma and me with the three kids. The older two were wearing floaties and running around the dock, while our youngest, Henry, was playing in the sandbox about 20 feet from shore. As my wife padded off down the cottage road, I had the brilliant idea to give the two older kids water guns. As it turned out, this was not a very good move. The first thing my son did was shoot my daughter in the face (because that's his idea of a really good time). My daughter is no shrinking violet, so she shot him right back, also in the face. What ensued was an all-out brawl.

As the fighting intensified, my mother and I became entirely engrossed in resolving the conflict. Eventually we got the two kids calmed down. They got time-outs, and they took their places sitting quietly on the dock. At this point, my mom said, "Where's Henry?" and all of a sudden I noticed that it was completely silent.

This was unusual. Henry is a loud kid. Plus, he couldn't walk yet, only crawl. So he couldn't have gone far, right? "He must be in the shed," said my mom. We ran to the shed. He wasn't there. We started calling out, "Henry, where are you?" Thirty seconds passed. A minute. We still didn't hear anything.

On one side of us was forest covering a steep hillside. On the other was the lake. Henry couldn't swim. My mom ran to check the other buildings. "Maybe he went into your sister's cottage?" she wondered. I acted on the worst-case scenario. The water. I went all the way to one side of the property, got in the thigh-deep water, and started working my way along the rocky shoreline, scrambling over the sharp rocks.

We were shouting Henry's name frantically enough that people from the other side of the lake got in their boats and drove over, calling out, "Is everything okay?"

I replied, "No, we've lost my baby." And as they started coming to help us look, I heard the sweetest sound in the world: Henry crying out from my sister's deck. Somehow he'd managed to crawl about 100 yards through the forest and get up onto her deck.

Whew.

From this period of just 8 to 10 minutes, two things really stuck with me. The first is that every time I had to check under one of the three docks on our shoreline, an image spontaneously came to mind of my son, in his blue bathing suit, floating under the dock. Holding that image meant I really had to force myself to look underneath. Deep breath. Look under the dock. Not there. Move on. The second thing is a consciousness that this could be the day my entire life changes. My wife went out for a run and left me with the kids. If Henry was truly gone, this was it: the demarcation line between the life I had and the life I was going to have from there on out.

This is an extreme example. There are few, if any, experiences in life that compare to losing a child. And yet, the hallmarks of this story—my pounding heart, a racing mind focused on all of the potential dangers, intense emotions—play out to varying degrees in situations ranging from sales presentations to crucial examinations. When the stakes are important enough, we feel pressure.

At the heart of this book is a simple but surprisingly powerful question: What's the most pressure you've ever been under?

I discovered the power of this question accidentally. The consulting firm I run, Third Factor, has focused on pressure for 30 years, and I spend a lot of my time delivering workshops and speeches on resilience to groups around the world. I started asking "What's the most pressure you've ever been under?" as a conversation starter when I was sitting around a table with participants at a break or over lunch. I quickly realized that this question was like a portal into a world of incredible experiences. Very early on, I asked this question at a dinner, and the man beside me—whom I had just met—told me about realizing he had screwed things up with the love of his life. After an on-again, off-again relationship, they had broken up. Almost a year later, he couldn't stop thinking about it, realized he had made a mistake, and decided to go all-in, buying a diamond ring from Van Cleef & Arpels and showing up at her door unannounced with two dozen roses and a marriage proposal. She opened the door and said, "What the hell are you doing here?" and he had seconds to convince her to let him in, and one shot at getting a yes. For him, that was the most pressure he'd ever been under. As we chatted, he happily filled me in on their 18 years of marriage, and the triplets (yes, triplets) they had raised together.

As I realized the remarkable experiences and wisdom that existed on the other side of this question, I started asking it more and probing deeper. I followed up on my initial query by digging to see what I could learn about both the situation and productive and unproductive responses to it, asking questions like:

- What made it so high-pressure?
- What did you do?
- What helped?
- What didn't help?
- What did other people do? Did that help?
- How did going through this change you?

This book is the result of what I learned from asking these questions over and over again—asking elite athletes, navy SEALs, and emergency doctors, but also ordinary people balancing the pressures we all face. I learned that pressure has patterns, and that those patterns repeat. That some things really help under pressure and others don't. That the things that help in peak pressure moments are often profoundly unhelpful for pressure over the long haul, and vice versa. That things like time management are actually pressure traps. That our biology can easily sabotage us with unproductive responses rooted in ancient stress responses.

I also learned, again and again, that pressure—uncomfortable though it may be—is an invaluable ally. The power of pressure can propel us to new peaks of performance and higher levels of development.

We are all working toward some vision of our future: treading a path toward achieving the things we need to achieve—sales targets, project milestones, making our mortgage payments—while at the same time creating a life that is meaningful and full of joy. And as we do this, pressure is our constant companion. Pressure is inherent in the journey of life because pressure is inherent in the journey of human growth and development. Simply put, if we are going to do things we haven't done before, we are going to experience pressure. Years ago, Thomas Carlyle memorably said, "No pressure, no diamonds." He was right. Pressure isn't just a nasty by-product of life, it's an essential input into high performance. A life well lived requires pressure.

And yet pressure is a double-edged sword. During the World Junior Hockey Championships a few years back, Nike put their signature spin on the link between pressure and performance. Through a barrage of TV ads, they declared "Pressure is power." There is wisdom in that slogan: power can heat your house, but it can also burn it down. Ultimately, pressure is a form of energy. And in the modern world, our bodies are receiving more of this energy than ever before. Far from being energizing, intense pressure can lead just as easily to anxiety, overwhelm, and exhaustion.

With this book, I'll show you that the solution isn't to insulate yourself from pressure, but rather to channel the power inherent in pressure toward beneficial responses—things that lead us to higher performance and personal growth, instead of sleepless nights and sapped energy.

So let's get started.

PART 1

UNDERSTANDING PRESSURE

—

CHAPTER 1

THE PRESSURE EQUATION

THE INTERPLAY OF IMPORTANCE, UNCERTAINTY, AND VOLUME

Curt Cronin is the former commanding officer of an elite US Navy SEAL team that conducts covert operations around the world on a moment's notice. Recently I asked him, "What's the most pressure you've ever been under?"

Cronin paused to consider his answer, which seems appropriate. After all, he has faced a lot of pressure throughout his career. He finished his special forces training just before 9/11. Ten years later, in a remote mountain valley in Afghanistan, 25 of his closest friends died after Taliban insurgents shot down their Chinook transport helicopter, in the single deadliest incident in Operation Enduring Freedom. But asked to describe the moment he was most under pressure, he told the story of the deployment that saw him, under cover of night, leading a large land-based team toward a target about half a mile away. Cronin was intentionally vague about some details, to preserve the mission's confidentiality, but during his leadership of the SEAL team, he frequently targeted Afghan compounds to capture or kill Taliban forces. Cronin was in the middle of his patrol, with special forces personnel dispersed all around him as the team moved toward the target, when suddenly they started taking fire.

Cronin felt extreme pressure to act, and act quickly. Because his troop had SEAL team soldiers and National Guard troops who were deployed with only two weeks' notice, "You end up with a myriad of components, including inexperienced soldiers," Cronin said, and the danger is that the longer action is delayed, the more the "cold creep of fear" starts to impact everyone. And so the pressure was on Cronin to act. To do something.

"There's multiple levels of this," Cronin said. "The first is, when you get shot at . . . everybody thinks, *How do I maneuver?* No, no, no, no, no. Step one, get down. If you don't get shot, you have an infinite amount of more time to figure this out, right? 'Cause when you hear the bullet crack past your head, that means . . . the good news is, you didn't get hit by that one, the bad news is, they shot and you didn't know they were aiming at you. So, step two, start to figure out where the fire's coming from and then, step three, begin . . . to act."

In this case, Cronin called in two support helicopters to rain fire down on their attackers.

"It might have been the second- or third-best choice," Cronin recalled. "But the fact that the decision was made—that made it the best choice."

In that moment of greatest pressure, Cronin believes he provided "the context and the confidence that allows people to continue to execute according to the plan." The gambit worked. The helicopters repelled the attack, and moments later Cronin's team was able to take the offensive and achieve their objective.

This is an example of an extreme peak pressure moment—one that combines high stakes with tremendous uncertainty. Attacked by assailants who wanted to kill him and his soldiers, Cronin turned to one of the most effective tools we'll examine in the book: establishing control and taking direct action as quickly as possible. While most of us will never command an elite SEAL platoon, everyone faces uncertain moments with high stakes that can define the trajectory of our lives.

So, what's the most pressure you've ever been under?

I've asked this question to more than 1,000 people over the past 18 months—in big groups, in small groups, and in one-on-one interviews—and the answers have spanned the vast range of human experience.

Some people identify a specific moment of intense pressure: delivering a speech (or in one case a baby on the side of the road), taking a high-stakes exam, preparing to step onto the ice for an Olympic speed skating final (more on that later), or—more gravely—being in a school during an active shooter situation.

Others describe a period of time in their lives that was particularly pressurized: caring for a dying parent while pursuing a challenging career, months of uncertainty at work after the company was acquired by a larger organization, or the dawning realization that their career was becoming obsolete.

There is a lot that is different across these situations. Some are almost entirely personal, while others are about work life. Some occurred when people were young; others, much later in life. Some involved literal life-and-death situations, while in others the stakes were a fair bit lower (even if they didn't feel like it at the time). And yet, across all of the situations I've examined, certain commonalities exist. They all are marked by some combination of three fundamental factors: high importance, high uncertainty, and high volume.

This combination of importance, uncertainty, and volume forms what I call the pressure equation, which is both a way of understanding pressure *and* a strategy for taking action on the circumstances that create pressure in our lives.

THE PRESSURE EQUATION
PRESSURE = IMPORTANCE × UNCERTAINTY × VOLUME

Let's take a look at each element of the pressure equation in turn, starting with this surprisingly thorny question: What is pressure?

PRESSURE

When I started asking people to describe their highest-pressure moment, one of my first epiphanies involved the realization that pressure can occur in a remarkable number of different human experiences. I heard stories about people throwing up from anxiety in the moments before they had to take an important exam. One person told me about discovering a loved one who had died by suicide. A business executive talked about facing down disruptive competition that threatened to bankrupt her firm.

Someone else described the moment he realized he had swum too far out from shore in a suddenly choppy ocean.

These different examples raise a pretty fundamental question: Are all of these situations examples of pressure? And what is pressure, really? How is it different from stress, fear, or grief? As you might expect, there are few "right" answers to these questions. All of human experience is largely subjective. When I have butterflies in my stomach, am I excited or nervous? These words are labels that we apply to an entire bundle of physical sensations. In fact, research from Alison Brooks at Harvard, among others, has shown that an ability to label these physical sensations productively (saying "I'm excited" instead of "I'm nervous," for example) can change our subjective experience of events, and therefore our responses.

But based on the research I've conducted over the last 18 months, I'd suggest that what distinguishes pressure from other states like stress, fear, or grief is the need to *do something*.

We often use the words "stress" and "pressure" interchangeably, but they aren't exactly the same. Consider a basketball game. Anyone who has ever watched a team they really care about play in a meaningful game has experienced stress. My wife is a hugely devoted Toronto Raptors fan. She cares so much about the team that she frequently has to leave the room and receive game updates by text message during the playoffs. The stress is too much for her to bear. Pressure, however, is *playing* in the game. It's not just an investment in the outcome, it's an ability to impact the outcome.

There is similar daylight between fear, grief, and pressure. It is awful to learn that a loved one has died by suicide. That's a discovery that will be accompanied by tremendous grief, and possibly anger. Pressure, however, is needing to phone up the loved one's relatives and describe what has happened in a way that is empathetic and compassionate. And so I'd like to offer up the following definition of pressure as distinct from related concepts like fear or grief:

> PRESSURE IS THE NEED TO ACT IN THE
> FACE OF IMPORTANT, UNCERTAIN CIRCUMSTANCES.

This brings us to the next component of the equation, and the first one on the other side of the equal sign: importance.

IMPORTANCE

The first driver of pressure is importance because, quite simply, if something doesn't matter to you, it won't create pressure. When I buy a lottery ticket, the outcome is highly uncertain, but my downside is comparatively unimportant, at just $5, so I don't agonize as the balls are drawn. Conversely, if a situation is important enough, even if the outcome is 99% certain, that last 1% can create immense distress. Consider how you would feel if you were being wheeled down a hospital corridor to get surgery with a 1% fatality rate.

During one of the many presentations I've given about the pressure equation, someone once asked me, "If importance is the primary factor in the pressure equation, why does work I don't even think is important create pressure?" This astute observation leads to a key point: it's not the importance of the task that matters; it's the importance of the outcome. Presumably, holding down a job is important to you and therefore, regardless of whether the work itself is important to you, you feel the pressure of doing a good job.

Similarly, what matters is the subjective importance you place on a situation. Regardless of how an outside observer might see the stakes, if your brain has coded the outcome as "important," the situation will create pressure. In many cases, the pressure stems in large part from ego-driven, manufactured importance, where one part of your internal narrative may involve the thought, *If I mess this up, everyone will think I'm an idiot.* As we will explore in Chapter 5, an ability to separate what is truly important from artificial or ego-driven stakes is at the heart of de-escalating and nailing peak pressure moments.

UNCERTAINTY

Any sufficiently important situation will be accompanied by some level of pressure, but what creates intense pressure is a combination of both importance and uncertainty. Curt Cronin's story from his deployment illustrates this blend particularly acutely in a crucial moment, but uncertainty can also play out over the longer term and slowly corrode our resilience.

Michelle Segal (not her real name) was a recent participant in the resilience program I teach at Queen's Smith School of Business. Like many people in the program, she had enrolled because she was dealing with a fair amount of pressure in her life. Also like many people I meet who are under significant pressure, you would never know she was carrying a heavy burden.

She was an active participant in the class, cheerful at breaks, and easy to talk to.

As the day reached an end, she came up to the front of the room. We talked about what she was going through at work. Eight months before, her employer, an agribusiness company, had been acquired by a larger organization based in Europe. As with any merger, the organizations were looking to find "synergies"—a wonderful consulting word that most often means "people to fire." Inevitably, a merger creates uncertainty, with everyone looking at their neighbor and wondering who will make the cut. In this case, rather than diffuse the uncertainty, the acquiring company had actually ratcheted it up, putting out a message to let Segal and her colleagues know that, at some point in the future, the teams focused on regulatory affairs would be merged and that only 8 of the current 13 staff members would be retained. From the note, Segal knew she was competing directly with her counterpart in the acquiring company—and that only one of them would have a job once the restructuring was complete.

The situation was making it hard for Segal to focus on her work. Hers was a highly specialized skill set. Few jobs like hers existed in Toronto. If she lost her position, she'd almost certainly have to relocate to a different city to work for another company. She'd have to move her family. Her husband might have to find new work. Or she might never work again. The instability was making it difficult to function. The pressure created by the constant background hum of uncertainty and pressure was affecting her job performance.

The pressure created by uncertainty is inextricably linked to importance—hence the first multiplication sign in the equation *pressure = importance × uncertainty × volume*. When events are unimportant or of modest importance, uncertainty can actually create enjoyment or anticipation. Consider the act of reading a novel or watching a television program. We don't want to know the end—we require the uncertainty to keep us enthralled. Similarly, Ayelet Fishbach, a professor of behavioral science and marketing at the University of Chicago, demonstrated that, counterintuitively, people would invest more effort in a task when the task's payout was uncertain. As she noted in an interview with *The Atlantic*: "It's exciting when the stakes are not huge. We try to keep the stakes small enough so excitement doesn't at any point turn into some terror. We don't assume people would like their salary to be uncertain. It's the small uncertainties."

As we'll see in Chapter 6, when the stakes rise to the level of Segal's ordeal—potential job loss, relocating the family—the human brain experiences the uncertainty as a sensation similar to physical pain. We are therefore wired to flee to certainty in these types of situations. When we can't, or won't, flee, we feel pressure.

VOLUME

We experience pressure at the intersection of importance and uncertainty. But what can make pressure relentless—especially in the modern world—is a third variable: volume.

I work with the Canadian Paralympic Committee (CPC), the organization that oversees Canada's Paralympic movement and orchestrates Team Canada's mission to the Games every two years. One of the things I like best about the CPC is that they doggedly pursue highly ambitious goals, the foremost of which is to lead Canada's ascent to becoming a world-leading Paralympic nation. That is a big goal for a country of 35 million people competing against countries 20 to 30 times our size, some of whom have a macabre "advantage" over Canada in that they have experienced conflict or natural disasters that give them a much larger pool of people with disabilities from which to draw.

A little while ago a new board of directors was elected, and one of the first things they requested from the executive team was a better scorecard. "We need to understand how we will know if we are moving toward world leading," one board member said. "What are the key metrics we should be tracking?"

I gathered the executive team to hammer out the first draft of a response. Before we designed the scorecard itself, the first question we asked ourselves was: What are all the things that could go on that scorecard? I asked each person to write out all of the metrics tracked by the CPC, one per Post-it Note, then stick them up on the wall to serve as a starting point.

Each person on the team immediately put pen to paper, and Post-it Notes started to dot the walls. In the span of five minutes— when I finally called mercy—189 Post-it Notes were stuck up on the wall, representing metrics from "number of gold medals" all the way to "staff satisfaction with IT." Just from memory alone, this team could think of 189 things in the organization that were both important enough and uncertain enough that they were being actively measured.

One. Hundred. And. Eighty. Nine.

This to me is a physical manifestation of the state of the pressure equation in the modern world—a staggering volume of important, uncertain things that take up both time and mental space, consciously or unconsciously.

Now, if you are like the many people with whom I have shared this story over the past year, you are probably not shocked by this. In fact, you may have just as many or more metrics in your organization. But it goes without saying that no team of people, no matter how capable or well-meaning, can truly attend to 189 things—which means that inevitably some of these important, uncertain items will migrate to the periphery, creating pressure each time you think of them and feel the sting of guilt over their neglect.

At the start of every workshop on resilience that my team and I conduct, we always put the following question to the class: What challenges or pressures are you currently facing that

- impair your performance?
- drain your physical energy?
- emotionally exhaust you?
- cause you anxiety?
- take away the fun?
- keep you rushing?

Volume—or its alter-ego, lack of time—is the first thing people mention more than 90% of the time. And it's never in just one facet of life. It's taking care of work and getting the kids to school on time. It's balancing self-care with elder care. It's trading off success at work with meaningful relationships outside of work. Volume permeates every nook and cranny of our lives. And it is only increasing.

The more volume we acquire, the more acutely we feel pressure—and the more likely we are to seek time-management skills for help. Paradoxically, however, time management can actually make the pressure worse, not better, as we will see in Chapter 8.

THE PARADOX OF PRESSURE

So, what's the most pressure you've ever been under? Take a second and actually think about it. If you're like most people I've interviewed, a moment or period in your life will quickly come to mind. Think about that situation. Was it important? Was it uncertain? Were you juggling a lot of balls? My suspicion is that, as you consider your scenario, you will answer yes to at least two of those questions—and perhaps all three.

When importance, uncertainty, and volume collide, a number of things happen to us as human beings. When I heard Henry cry after I lost him at the cottage, I had to double over to recover. My chest was heaving and my heart was pounding. My body reacted to the pressure like I was running a sprint. Periods of intense importance and uncertainty can create extreme physiological effects. Michelle Segal, facing down months of uncertainty over her job security, didn't breathe like she was sprinting, but her physiology had changed too. She wasn't sleeping as soundly as she had previously, and there was a lot going on with her body's levels of adrenaline and cortisol, which we'll explore further in Chapter 2.

Beyond physiology, pressure affects our emotions and thought patterns. It causes our field of attention to narrow, impeding our ability to absorb information. We retreat to our biases. Pressure makes it more challenging to be empathetic, creative, and agile. Ironically, the abilities we lose if we don't manage ourselves when under pressure—empathy, creativity, learning—underpin some of the most effective responses to pressure. This is the paradox of pressure: our body's default response to pressure robs us of the very abilities that can most help us manage our response to pressure.

This physiological reality isn't new, but in the modern world all three elements of the pressure equation are increasing, which means the paradox of pressure is coming into play more than ever before. Most of us are dealing with a volume of inputs that would have felt baffling to prior generations: emails, instant messages, Slack channels, and social media notifications combine to create a constant stream of information—almost all of which is invested with a sense of importance, whether deserved or not.

Added on top of this constant hum is an unprecedented volume of bigger changes: the rise of digitization and automation has created significant uncertainty around job security. Massive political uncertainty is rocking the Western world. Demographic changes mean many of us are caring for aging parents within an overburdened health-care system.

Underpinning the tools described in in this book is a recognition that many high-pressure situations have unique features. While multiple factors are most often at play, one part of the equation tends to dominate. Perhaps you were fixated on the stakes— on how important this event was to your life. Or perhaps the outcome was so uncertain that you couldn't stop thinking about whether you might "lose." Or perhaps even though no one thing was a life-or-death matter, the sheer volume of demands created a level of pressure that prevented you from sleeping or focusing on what mattered most.

Leo Tolstoy famously said in *Anna Karenina* that "Happy families are all alike; every unhappy family is unhappy in its own way." The same is true when it comes to pressure: low-pressure situations are all reasonably similar, but each high-pressure situation has its own fingerprint. The good news is, after exploring hundreds of high-pressure moments, I can tell you that they follow a set of predictable patterns.

Understanding how the pressure equation applies to a particular situation helps us to determine the best strategy to manage the pressure. For example, if the pressure I'm facing is due to acute importance, a perspective skill will typically provide the greatest help. If the pressure is predominantly due to uncertainty, I may want to turn to direct action. We'll learn more about how to know which tool to use, and when, in Part 2.

PEAK PRESSURE MOMENTS AND THE LONG HAUL

At one particularly low moment in my life, I panicked at a build-your-own-salad bar and—under pressure to place my order—paired a salad containing buffalo chicken with poppy seed dressing. A terrible choice. You may wonder why you have chosen to read a book on pressure written by someone who finds a salad bar overly stressful. But what I realized that day is that certain flavors work well together and some, like spicy buffalo chicken and creamy poppy seed dressing, do not.

Broadly speaking, pressure can be found in two flavors: peak pressure moments—short, violent bursts of extreme importance and uncertainty—and the long haul—periods of grinding volume mixed with importance and uncertainty along the way.

Moving beyond simply enduring pressure and toward using it as a source of fuel requires managing both forms. And just like my salad bar experience, there are certain ingredients that work in one situation that decidedly will not work in another.

For example, when we are facing a peak pressure moment characterized by intense uncertainty, our best option is often to take immediate direct action on something we can influence—taming uncertainty in any way possible to bring back a sense of control. When Curt Cronin called in the helicopters, he didn't care if that was the second- or third-best option; managing pressure in that moment was all about acting right away. Over the long haul, however, attempting to control all of the uncertainty in our lives as quickly as possible is a recipe for burnout. What we need to do, in fact, is to learn to accept or even embrace the inevitable uncertainties that accompany life.

These seeming paradoxes are part of what makes exploring the pressure equation so much fun. As we examine how to navigate importance, uncertainty, and volume over both the long haul and in our peak pressure moments, you'll start to see that a beautiful symmetry exists in the patterns of pressure.

CHAPTER 2

BLOOD, SWEAT, AND BREATH

HOW YOUR BODY HANDLES PRESSURE

Rationally or irrationally, we are feeling more pressure now than ever. And when we feel pressure, our bodies react—often in ways that undermine our ability to respond productively. We often think of pressure as an external force, something that is inherent in a situation: we feel pressure because of quarterly sales targets that are imposed on us by management; we feel pressure because we need to pass a professional exam; we feel pressure because our team is counting on us to hit a free throw. The reality is that pressure is an internal experience. When we are sitting alone in our house at night and hear a strange noise in the basement, a chain of events can unfold inside us that causes us to feel pressure, regardless of whether there is anyone down there. Put another way, two people can be in the same situation—standing on stage, at the start of a race, or in the middle of a particularly intense family game night—and one can feel pressure while the other is entirely carefree. Pressure is found in our response to a situation, not the situation itself.

In Chapter 1, I defined pressure as the need to act in important, uncertain circumstances. Here's the thing: the need to act can be exciting to some and terrifying to others. And the degree to which each of us perceives a situation as either important or uncertain is highly subjective and open to manipulation.

THE PRESSURE PROCESS

What happens inside us to create the feeling of pressure? Like most internal processes, the short answer is: it's complicated. We know it involves our thought processes, our emotional state, and physical changes to our body, but while some aspects of how the internal experience of pressure arises are well understood, others are only just beginning to be explored. That said, let's start with the basics: the sympathetic nervous system.

The nervous system has two main subsystems: the central nervous system, which comprises the brain and spinal cord, and the peripheral nervous system, which is the web of nerves that extends throughout the body to ferry information to and from the central nervous system. The peripheral system is again divided into two major subdivisions: the somatic system, which is associated with voluntary actions like moving your leg or grasping with your hand, and the autonomic system (ANS), which handles things that are typically thought to be outside of our direct control—salivation, peripheral vision, sensory gating, and so on. The ANS is where we want to pause, because it's what regulates your physiological responses to stressors. The ANS has two main components: the sympathetic system and parasympathetic system.

The sympathetic system gets your body activated for stress while the parasympathetic system does the reverse—it reduces activation and helps your body return to a state more suitable to regular moment-to-moment performance. You can think of these two systems as somewhat like the gas and brake pedals in a car. One floods the system with fuel and revs the engine, the other slows things down and helps you dump excess energy.

BIOFEEDBACK AND NEUROFEEDBACK

What happens inside us when the gas pedal gets pressed is becoming increasingly well understood thanks to advances in two related fields: biofeedback, which gives us a window into what happens to us physically when we're under pressure, and neurofeedback, which aims to do the same for what happens cognitively.

Dr. Penny Werthner is the dean of kinesiology at the University of Calgary, a sport psychologist, and a pioneer in the use of biofeedback and neurofeedback to help athletes perform under pressure. When I sat down with her—first by phone and then in her office beside the Olympic oval built for the 1988 Calgary Games—she talked about how these new tools have changed our understanding of pressure. First and foremost, we have begun to understand that the experience of pressure is both a psychological and a physical one. "For years, what we've done in the field of sport psychology is talk about the cognitive process. For years, it has been all about the psychological side without really considering the physiology that goes along with it." The cordoning off of pressure into the domain of psychology, or "mental performance," didn't jive with Dr. Werthner's own experiences as an elite athlete, or with what she was seeing in her work with athletes—many of whom were talking to her about feeling physically tight or short of breath. In the compartmentalized world of sport, however, those were considered problems for others who were focused on the physical side of performance—remedied through a pre-race massage, better conditioning, or work on mobility and flexibility. "In our field of sport psychology, we've always talked about the psychological without anything else. And of course, all of our physiologists in sport talk about the physiology without really considering the brain."

Starting to work with bio- and neurofeedback in the 1990s forced Dr. Werthner to confront some of the biases she was holding as a sport psychologist. "Biofeedback and neurofeedback are really just tools to show one person what actually happens to them under stress. And for sure when I started, I thought the EEG part—the neurological part—would be the most important, because in sport psychology we talk about focus all the time. And yet it became very clear to me that the physiology was also incredibly relevant." That's because the mind and body end up becoming mutually reinforcing systems when under pressure. "If you're doing something incredibly important—whether that's an Olympic final or an important proposal—most of us start to think, *If I screw this up, I'm toast,* or something similar. And the second we think those kind of thoughts we immediately change physiologically."

PHYSIOLOGICAL CHANGES

How we change under pressure is both individual and situational. In general, however, the sympathetic nervous system begins sending signals to the adrenal glands to produce adrenaline and cortisol, increasing your heart rate, dilating the bronchi in your lungs to allow for more oxygen intake, inhibiting salivation and digestion to preserve energy, ramping up sweat to dump excess heat, and constricting blood flow to core organs—reducing peripheral skin temperature and circulation.

"Because pressure is an individual experience, biofeedback measures five modalities," explains Dr. Werthner. "First, breathing—because when we get stressed most of us breathe faster and in the top of our chest. Second, heart rate. Third, some of us sweat more, so skin conductance is another modality. Fourth, shoulders come up and muscles get tighter, so we measure muscle tension. Of course, in sport, that is a critical piece—it totally screws up performance. And finally, peripheral temperature. Everything else we want to bring down, but on temperature we want to bring it up, because we're measuring it on the fingers or the toes. We want to see the blood flowing everywhere, because when we go to 'fight or flight,' it's all going to go to get redirected to our heart." Pressure won't show up across all five modalities for everyone, but this gives everyone a chance to see their own pressure signature.

Figure 1 illustrates a biofeedback training session with an elite wrestler, undertaken by Kara Stelfox, my team's research and development lead for resilience. The session was divided into three components: two minutes of baseline measurement with no stimulus; six minutes of "pressure" during which the athlete visualized competing, with the audio of a prior wrestling match piped in to heighten the visceral sense of being there; and a four-minute recovery period. The entire time, Stelfox was monitoring heart rate (see top graph) and respiration rate (see bottom graph).

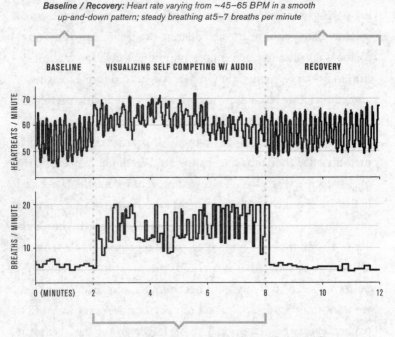

Baseline / Recovery: Heart rate varying from ~45–65 BPM in a smooth up-and-down pattern; steady breathing at 5–7 breaths per minute

Under pressure: Elevated heart rate with compressed and more erratic variability; erratic breathing that ranges from 10–20 breaths per minute

FIGURE 1: *Biofeedback training session #1*

In the first and third sections (baseline and recovery), the athlete is in a state of high "coherence"—a high-performance state in which the rise and fall of breathing and heart rate are synchronized. You can see this in the smooth up-and-down wave pattern of her heart rate and her steady, slow breathing at 5 to 7 breaths per minute. As an elite athlete, she has trained herself to breathe slowly (typical respiration rates are closer to 12 to 15 breaths per minute), and she is able to recover to baseline incredibly quickly at the eight-minute mark. This is the parasympathetic system doing its job.

But when the pressure hits, even simulated pressure like visualizing a competition, you can see a number of significant changes: quicker and far more erratic breathing, an elevated heart rate, and—crucially—smaller and more erratic heart rate variability. In short: no coherence.

Figure 2 shows the same session again but looked at through the lens of "peripheral temperature." Remember what Dr. Werthner said: as the body's sympathetic nervous system activates, even though the heart is pumping faster and harder, the body conserves blood flow for the core, and so circulation to peripheral areas like the fingers and toes drops, causing their temperature to fall.

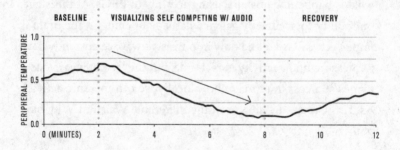

FIGURE 2: *Biofeedback training session #2*

Again, you can see that as the pressure progresses from two minutes to eight minutes, peripheral temperature takes a nosedive. Blood isn't flowing nearly as freely as it was before the pressure hit. And even after a four-minute recovery period, it still hasn't returned to baseline levels. This decline in peripheral temperature is akin to what happens in extreme cold: the body conserves energy by rationing blood flow to support essential systems and organs.

We'll get into the performance challenges that accompany this physiological state soon, but what I want you to take away here is that even highly trained athletes, when facing simulated pressure in a controlled environment, see dramatic changes to their bodies. These physical responses are hardwired into us at a very basic level and have been reinforced over tens of thousands of years of evolution. They are not easily countered.

NEUROLOGICAL CHANGES

What about the brain? Whereas biofeedback gives us information on the body's responses to pressure, neurofeedback helps us see what is happening upstairs, using an array of EEGs. At this stage, our ability to accurately gauge what is happening in the brain is imperfect. EEGs are the only noninvasive way we currently have to measure brain activity in real time, but the lack of invasiveness comes at a cost in terms of how locally we can measure activity. As Tim Urban, the creator of the incredible Wait But Why blog puts it:

> Imagine that the brain is a baseball stadium, its neurons are the members of the crowd, and the information we want is, instead of electrical activity, vocal cord activity. In that case, EEG would be like a group of microphones placed outside the stadium, against the stadium's outer walls. You'd be able to hear when the crowd was cheering and maybe predict the type of thing they were cheering about. You'd be able to hear telltale signs that it was between innings and maybe

whether or not it was a close game. You could probably detect when something abnormal happened. But that's about it.

So, standing outside the stadium walls, we can listen for different frequencies of electrical activity—what we call brain waves. Broadly speaking, there are four frequencies that an EEG can measure:

- **Delta waves** dominate during deep, dreamless sleep.
- **Theta waves** accompany lighter parts of the sleep cycle and a daydreaming state.
- **Alpha waves** are associated with a meditative, lucid state free from thought—the rest and recovery state for the awake brain.
- **Beta waves** are observed when we are awake, alert, and thinking.

Not all beta waves are created equal. Beta encompasses a broad range that spans 12–38 hertz. At the bottom end of the spectrum, the brain is in "fast idle" thought—or musing. When high beta waves (22–38 hertz) are dominant, it is a sign that we have moved into something akin to overdrive, with the brain continually processing. This is a highly activated state that many of us are familiar with, as it accompanies tossing and turning in bed while your mind races as you desperately try to fall asleep.

For most of us, the body's activation in response to pressure is accompanied by an increase in high beta waves as the brain moves to a similarly active state. As Dr. Werthner says: "What happens is that after we say to ourselves *This is so important*, we change physiologically—but then it rolls back up to the brain, and we can't stop thinking it's really important. Then we start to do dumb things. Athletes fall when they never fall. They come out of the blocks faster than they've ever come out of the blocks and hit the first hurdle—and they're out. And it's usually because they start overthinking the skills as opposed to just letting it happen."

THE BRAIN-GUT CONNECTION

In Dr. Werthner's telling, the brain's framing of an event as important activates the body, which then rebounds up to the brain and starts a reinforcing feedback loop. Now, the direction of this loop is the subject of some debate. There are, broadly speaking, two tribes: the cognitivists, such as Dr. Werthner, who contend that pressure begins with thought processes (*Oh my goodness, this is so important*), and those who believe that our sympathetic nervous system responds precognitively to pressure: our muscles tense up, our heart rate increases, and *then* our brain labels the physical sensations that arise spontaneously in our body as pressure, fear, or anxiety, which reinforces the feedback loop.

For our practical purposes, the direction of initial cause and effect are largely irrelevant, because however the gas pedal gets pressed, once it's initiated, our thoughts, emotions, and physiology are all interconnected and influence each other.

The nervous system is continuously relaying information in both directions—from brain to body and vice versa. This occurs through many channels, but one of the most important is the vagus nerve. The longest nerve in the body, the vagus stretches from the brain stem to the colon. It is a vital link between the viscera and the brain, constantly conveying information on the status of our gut, lungs, and heart to our brain. The vagus nerve ensures that our brain knows exactly how activated our body is—that our heart is pounding and our stomach is in knots. For the purposes of managing pressure, it is vital to understand this connection, because in extreme situations our body's messages can overwhelm thought-based interventions. To go back to one opening example in this chapter, if I try to use self-talk to tell myself "Don't be silly, there's no one in the basement—everything's okay," but my vagus nerve is telling my brain that my heart is pounding, my digestion has slowed down, and my breathing is ragged, guess which message the brain listens to? That's right: the body, which is saying loudly that everything is not okay.

Heather Watt is the chief of staff for Christine Elliott, the minister of health for the province of Ontario. A veteran of business and politics, Watt helped run Elliott's campaign for the leadership of the Conservative Party, and then moved into the chief of staff role when Elliott became minister of health. When the COVID-19 pandemic erupted in early 2020, Watt was immediately thrust into one of the highest-pressure jobs in the country. "The word 'unprecedented' gets thrown around a lot—but I think we can all agree that these circumstances have been truly unprecedented." Because she was responsible for advising on policy with life-and-death implications for 14.5 million people, the weight of her portfolio was significant. "The magnitude of the responsibility, combined with complete uncertainty about anything, was not comfortable. We're used to that discomfort a little bit, but it escalated dramatically under the circumstances, because even the most intelligent public health officials that we could find, epidemiologists, etcetera, really didn't know what we were dealing with."

As if this wasn't enough on its own, Watt was seven months pregnant with her third child when the government of Ontario made the decision to declare a state of emergency on March 17. The demands of an already demanding job escalated significantly: "We all work really hard, we all know that, it's what we signed up for—weekends, nights—and that's all good. This was seven days a week, 20 hours a day, of just trying to wrap our arms around what we knew as an incredible public health crisis, and it really felt like not working was wasting time that we didn't have."

Unsurprisingly, in the midst of this incredible pressure cooker, Watt began to experience the physical impacts of stress. "There were more than a few nights where it was very, very difficult to go from the amount of work that we were doing, at the velocity with which it was all occurring, to then falling asleep. I'd get home after midnight—again, at eight months pregnant—and try to make sure that I've eaten something, had some water, and then lie in bed trying to sleep."

In the end, only one thing worked: deep breathing. "I remember one particular night when I got into bed, I actually was shaking—like I was just buzzing from pressure, limited sleep, probably not enough calories, probably being pregnant, all of those things coming together, and I just could not calm my nervous system down. There was honestly only one thing that got me to sleep that night. I just thought, *Heather, take 10 deep breaths, and then do it again, and then do it again.*"

In extremely heightened circumstances, we must be able to get our body under control if we are going to make headway on what is happening upstairs. And focusing on our breathing is far and away the best way to accomplish that—which is why we will explore it in more detail in Chapter 6 as a way to establish control in the midst of uncertainty.

Now, the train runs both ways. If I can't get my thoughts under control—if I'm always focused on how important something is, or what's at stake, or how stressed I'm feeling—it will be impossible for my body to return to a high-performance state. That is why how we frame events is so vital to managing pressure, a thread that runs through this book.

ATTENTIONAL TUNNELING

But why does it matter if your heart is pounding, if your breathing is quicker, or if your brain is racing in high beta? Well, it matters because it has a tremendous impact on your performance and, if you don't manage it over the long haul, your health. As Dr. Werthner said, one issue when our brain becomes highly active is that we start to overthink things. But there are other issues as well, relating to the crucial relationship between how activated our body is and the way our brain processes information or chooses to ignore it.

At all times, whether under pressure or not, our brain engages in the process of "sensory gating": constantly and automatically making decisions about what visual, auditory, and other sensory information to let in—and what to gate out. This is an essential function of the brain. If we were constantly aware of every place our clothing makes contact with our body, or of every conversation in a crowded restaurant, we would be incapacitated. In fact, a lack of sensory gating is one of the markers of schizophrenia.

When we move into an activated state, our sensory gating goes into overdrive. The amount of information our brain lets in—the stimuli we are capable of processing—shrinks. Most of us know this intuitively. If you're facing off with someone who is highly emotional, you naturally think, *This person can't hear me right now—they can't absorb what I'm saying. I need to wait until they calm down.*

This narrowed focus applies both externally and internally. Externally, our peripheral vision narrows so that we can only see what is right in front of us. We fail to hear sounds. In fact, in research done with 157 police officers involved in shootings, 84% reported diminished sound, 79% reported tunnel vision, and 52% reported memory loss for at least part of the event. One stated: "If it hadn't been for the recoil, I wouldn't have known my gun was working. Not only didn't I hear the shots, but afterward my ears weren't even ringing." Another noted, "I told the SWAT team the suspect was firing at me from down a long, dark hallway about 40 feet long. When I went back to the scene the next day, I was shocked to discover he had actually been only about 5 feet in front of me in an open room. There was no hallway."

These are extreme examples, but the same phenomenon happens to a lesser degree in more traditionally stressful situations. At the end of a sales call that didn't go well, a colleague might let you know in the debrief that you had allies around the table who were nodding and trying to support your position—but you were entirely focused on the one person across from you who wasn't buying in and was asking difficult questions. You got tunnel vision and missed information in the environment that could have helped you.

Internally, this attentional narrowing has the potential to lead to a variety of issues. First, it can rob us of access to our own skills and knowledge. I had one particularly acute personal experience with this in a job interview. It was a few years after graduating from business school and I was trying to make the leap from working in my family business to management consulting. For the most part, consulting firms hire directly out of the graduating classes at universities. To come in with a few years of work experience puts you outside of traditional recruiting processes. I didn't have the marks to land interviews at the big-name firms when I graduated, but by 2007 I had done reasonably well and was able to get a couple of people to vouch for me and bring me into the recruiting process. I made it to the final round of interviews at Boston Consulting Group, one of the most prestigious firms out there, and I was sitting across the table from one of the partners in the Toronto office. It was my fourth interview of the day, and this one was a "case-based interview." In this instance, that meant I was given the following challenge: "Your client is a big-box retailer looking to review its product strategy. Specifically, they are looking to determine which product categories—sporting goods, hard goods, automotive, etcetera—they should stay in, get out of, or get into." Based on this premise, my job was to ask questions to get the information I needed to make a recommendation by the end of the interview. All things considered, it's a pretty decent simulation of what being a consultant is like.

For 30 minutes, I asked questions. I knew they weren't good questions. She knew they weren't good questions. At the end of 30 painful minutes, I made a half-hearted recommendation on what the company should do. We stood up and shook hands, and I walked out. I knew I wasn't getting the job. She knew I wasn't getting the job. It was a long, painful walk down the hallway to the elevator.

The second the elevator doors closed, all the questions I should have asked began flooding into my brain. One in particular hit me like a thunderbolt. With a four-year business degree and three years of work experience I hadn't asked the single most basic question: "How profitable are each of the product categories currently?" I was gobsmacked. If I could think of these questions 30 seconds after the interview, how come I couldn't think of them during the interview? Quite simply, my focus got too narrow and I couldn't access the information stored in my brain. Just as the police officer couldn't see the walls or hear the bullets, I couldn't see the questions that were floating just outside the tunnel vision in my head.

Aside from the issue of straight recall, attentional tunneling has a number of unfortunate side effects. First, it restricts our capacity for empathy. Empathy requires an ability to hold two different stories simultaneously—your own and the perspective of another person. It's very difficult to do that when your attention becomes overly narrow. Narrowed focus makes it much more likely that high-pressure situations involving other people will escalate as each person retreats to their own perspective and biases.

Second, attentional tunneling blocks us from absorbing new information. A big part of performance under pressure is the ability to adjust in response to new data. As we start to get more activated, adapting becomes very difficult and we rely on the information we brought into the situation.

Third, it shuts down our capacity for exploration. Research has shown that introducing pressure in the form of monetary incentives improves performance on routine tasks but significantly impairs performance on creative tasks because, as pressure rises, people are more likely to engage in "functional fixedness"—an unwillingness to deviate from one course of action and explore other alternatives. When we get really focused, we are much more likely to drive down a path we're already on.

Finally, as we get more and more activated, it becomes harder to learn new behaviors. Learning requires conscious attention, discipline, and willpower. As our energy level goes up, we revert to our default behaviors—those that are habitual and require very little attention—because that's all we can do with the small amount of attention we have.

RISKS OVER THE LONG HAUL

So far, we've talked mainly about moments of extreme pressure, in which the issues created by activation are mostly performance-oriented. To use the language of sport, we choke. Over the long haul of a high-pressure life, however, the issues that pressure can create aren't as tied to performance but manifest in more fundamental ways, impacting our life satisfaction, our relationships, and, ultimately, our health.

Decades ago, cardiologist and Harvard professor Dr. Herbert Benson first started unpacking the link between the continuous activation of the fight-or-flight response and the cardiac health of the people who were showing up at his practice. What he found, and compellingly wrote about in his blockbuster bestseller *The Relaxation Response*, was that when our bodies live in a continuously activated state, it has very real consequences for our health.

In particular, elevated levels of cortisol in our blood over time are linked to increased blood cholesterol, triglycerides, blood sugar, and blood pressure—all risk factors for heart disease. What begins as a momentary performance issue can turn into a life-changing health issue.

And it isn't just our bodies that suffer when moment-to-moment stressors become long-term pressure cookers. When we stay in an activated state over time, narrowed attention can become our brain's default. Think of all of the overwhelmed people who, in the midst of dealing with stressors at work, begin to let their self-care go or neglect their families. Their explanation is: "I just can't pay attention to that right now." When we are dominated by pressure, the volume of things vying for our attention across the different arenas of life can feel overwhelming. In order to survive, we necessarily focus on what we feel is most important. In the same way that I only remembered the information I needed to nail the job interview after the fact, it's often only after a heart attack or a divorce that people realize they had tunnel vision the whole time.

PRIMITIVE RESPONSES IN A MODERN WORLD

The human body is the single greatest organism, system—heck, thing—we know of. Through millions of years of continuous mutation and natural selection, every cell has been refined in the universe's greatest trial-and-error process to create an unparalleled marvel of engineering. So why on earth do we have all of these unbelievably counterproductive responses to pressure? How is it possible that we are equipped with a system that narrows our peripheral vision, shrinks our creativity, reduces our ability to recall important information, and robs us of empathy?

The answer is that evolution is a very slow process. The hardware we are equipped with evolved over the course of hundreds of thousands of years that were characterized by very different sources of pressure than most of us are faced with today. In the absence of intervention, our most primitive responses often dominate under pressure. These responses evolved to optimize for safety, predictability, and physical power in acutely stressful situations—the things that matter when you are hunting for food, facing a physical threat, or trying to figure out whether you should investigate that rustle in the bushes. Creativity, information recall, and empathy may be what we need in the midst of a big presentation that is slowly going very wrong, but they certainly weren't the things most correlated with survival under pressure over the total span of human existence.

In the midst of this mismatch, we must all act in the modern world, leading lives that will inevitably be accompanied by pressure along the way. We must cope with the fact that our default responses to pressure often rob us of the very tools necessary to thrive under stress. This is the paradox of pressure. And it's a paradox we must resolve if we are to nail the moments that matter and enjoy meaningful, healthy lives.

SIDESTEPPING THE DEFAULT RESPONSES

The secret to solving the paradox of pressure is to recognize that pressure isn't a set of external circumstances, it's an internal experience. And because it is an internal experience, we can change it.

I've talked a lot about what the research says when it comes to our default responses to pressure—but that word "default" is vital. We used to think the fight-or-flight response was the body's sole reaction to stress, but we now know it has a repertoire of responses. And unlike the inhibiting hallmarks of the fight-or-flight response, some of the other responses provide what are, in essence, superpowers. We've all heard stories of someone surging with adrenaline who lifts a car off an injured child. But what about people who, under pressure, reach out to build connections with others? People whose responses to pressure seem to elevate their capacity for empathy? Those who become more motivated, determined, inclusive, and creative? They all have one thing in common: they have side-stepped the default responses.

There are many ways to accomplish this. For example, if you make a conscious choice to see a situation as a challenge instead of a threat, your body produces less cortisol and your blood vessels expand rather than constrict, lowering your blood pressure and eliminating many of the sensory gating issues we talked about earlier. The simple act of saying "I'm excited" instead of "I'm nervous" when you feel the physical sensations of pressure has been shown to improve your ability to execute a challenge or creative task to the best of your abilities. And a massive research study of over 30,000 people at the University of Wisconsin, memorably summarized by leading stress researcher Kelly McGonigal in a TED Talk entitled "How to Make Stress Your Friend," showed that seeing stress as a positive thing instead of something harmful completely eliminated its long-term health impacts as measured by premature mortality.

In short, while external events may be out of your control, your internal response to those events isn't.

CHAPTER 3

BECOMING PRESSURE AMBIDEXTROUS

PERFORMANCE IN THE MOMENT AND OVER TIME

When we think about pressure, we typically think about moments: Curt Cronin taking enemy fire on deployment, a big sales presentation we need to nail to keep our career on track, a high-stakes exam that will impact where we go to university. But there's another form of pressure.

In 2019, with the Toronto Raptors up 3–1 in a best-of-seven series against the defending champion Golden State Warriors in the NBA Finals, Kyle Lowry sat at a press conference and was asked what pressure meant to him. A perennial all-star, and the de facto captain of the Raptors, Lowry was in the midst of one of the highest-pressure periods of his professional life. Before the season, the Raptors had traded his fellow star and best friend DeMar DeRozan to San Antonio in exchange for Kawhi Leonard, an injured superstar whom most saw (rightly, it turned out) as a hired gun brought in for one season to lead the team to victory. The team had asked Lowry to swallow the loss of his friend and surrender leadership of a team that had been "his" for the past five playoff seasons in service of hopefully breaking through to the biggest stage. Lowry had done all of that and, led by Kawhi, the team was on the verge of doing the impossible: beating the Warriors to secure Toronto's first-ever NBA Championship. On the eve of his first shot at a league championship, here is what Lowry told reporters pressure means to him:

> What my mom had to go through, what my grandmother had to go through, feeding myself, my brother, my cousin, my little cousin, my other little cousins. Going to work, getting up at five in the morning and [still] having a bowl of cereal sitting in the refrigerator with some milk [for me]. Being able to provide for me, my brother, and my family. That's pressure. That's pressure to me.

In what had to be one of the highest-pressure moments of Lowry's life, he didn't take the expected route when asked about pressure. He talked about enduring pressure over time. And while Lowry didn't bring home the championship in Game 5, he delivered an all-time performance in Game 6, scoring the Raptors' first 11 points to establish an early 11–2 lead, and eventually putting up 26 points and 10 rebounds to bring the first NBA Championship to Canada in the Raptors' 25th season. This is someone who understands pressure.

Pressure comes in many flavors. Importance, uncertainty, and volume can combine in an almost infinite number of ways. Sometimes, with enough importance, even the tiniest bit of uncertainty can create pressure. Other times, the sheer volume of what we're navigating creates pressure even if each individual item isn't hugely important to us. But broadly speaking, there are two major ways pressure manifests that we'll examine over the remainder of the book: *peak pressure moments*, like Lowry's performance in Game 6, and *the long haul* of pressure over time.

THE LONG HAUL

Jeremiah Brown is an unlikely Olympian. After graduating from university with a torn labrum that had ended his college football career, he moved back in with his parents. On August 17, 2008, he sat on his parents' couch and watched, enraptured, as the Canadian men's eight rowing crew triumphed over the British and American rowers to bring home gold. His athletic spirit rekindled, he made a bold promise to himself: "I will be on that podium in four years in London." There was only one problem: outside of a single disastrous one-hour experiment in a four-man boat the year before, he had never set foot in a rowing shell.

That small inconvenience did not hold Brown back. He found a job at TD Bank in Victoria, British Columbia—2,800 miles across the country and the home of the national team's training center. By a stroke of luck, at his company's holiday party in December 2008, he was pointed toward Doug White, the head coach of the Victoria City Rowing Club. When I sat down with Brown, he talked about how pivotal that first meeting with White was: "I remember looking at this guy with this baseball, leathery face, creased and wrinkled from all those years coaching on the water, and feeling like, I need this guy to believe in me. Because he knows what he's talking about." For the first time, Brown put into words what he was trying to achieve. "Doug looked at me, and he said, 'Jeremiah, what do you intend to do in this sport?' And for the first time, I vocalized it: 'Doug, I want to go to the Olympics, and I want to win a gold medal.' I just threw down the gauntlet." Staring across the table at a naive 22-year-old who had never taken a proper rowing stroke, White simply said, "Well, we don't have a lot of time. We better get to work."

"Rowing is a pain game," Brown would tell me later. And the period that followed was definitely one of pain—physical and psychological. He would wake up at 4:30 a.m., rolling out of a warm bed to make the icy drive to Elk Lake. In the dead of winter at 5:30 a.m., the rowers were on the water with LED lights affixed to their boats, bobbing in the pitch black. Following a grueling workout he would sprint to work, often arriving last, to the displeasure of his new boss. At lunch he would head down to the YMCA to get in a second workout, returning to work dripping with sweat. And finally, at the end of the day, he would head home, exhausted, to his partner, Amy, and their young son, Ethan.

In the midst of this demanding routine, his relationship with Amy unraveled. It was gut-wrenching and only added another layer of pressure to Brown's life. Not only was he holding down a full-time job and training twice a day, he was a single dad half the time and feeling profound guilt the other half.

The first major milestone on the path to Olympic glory was the National Championships in 2010. An exhausting period of increased training with White paid off: Brown finished second to Mike Braithwaite and nabbed a "D-Card" that entitled him to national development funding as an elite athlete. This was the golden ticket. The minimal funds it provided were just enough to allow Brown to take a leave of absence from his job at the bank and move to a full-time training regimen. Finishing second at Nationals also accomplished something else: it put him squarely on the radar of men's National Team head coach Mike Spracklen, who, in January of 2011, pulled Brown into the National Team training group.

Spracklen was a proven winner who had guided teams to the podium at six different Olympic Games. He was also the owner of a well-earned reputation for working athletes harder than they could possibly imagine. The uptick in training volume was immediate and brutal. Spracklen didn't believe in pacing in training—he demanded that every workout be done at full intensity. In the damp Victoria climate, the blood blisters on Brown's hands never turned to callouses. To avoid coating the handles of his oars with a mixture of blood and blister serum, he would Krazy Glue his wounds closed every day before his first training session. He existed under a constant cloud of physical pain—between the blisters on his hands and torn tendon sheaths in his fingers that couldn't fully heal without Brown taking a rest that would essentially disqualify him from competing for a seat in the boat, he was a mess.

But it was the psychological pressure that was the killer. With eight seats in the boat that would compete in 2012, and 20 rowers training with the National Team program, there was intense competition within the ranks, something that Spracklen encouraged. As they neared major competitions, they would routinely engage in "seat races" where one rower would be switched out of the boat for another to see what happened to the boat's time. If the boat got faster after you were swapped out, well . . . that wasn't good for you. Almost no one was safe, and the coach used the uncertainty around placement in the boat to fuel the competitive fire of the athletes.

The three grueling years Brown endured between his move to Victoria and the eventual London 2012 Games are an example of what I call the "long haul": a period of intense volume and pressure that is grinding and unrelenting. Often, the long haul is a period, like Brown's, that is building toward a peak pressure moment. In his case, that was the Olympic Games; for others, it could be months of work to secure a big client, the grind of developing and launching a new product, or preparing for a big presentation at a conference or a professional exam.

In other cases, long periods of pressure aren't building toward anything—they simply exist. This type of long haul can come on gradually, as additional sources of pressure are slowly layered on, one by one, until you realize you are no longer sleeping well at night or are feeling emotionally overwhelmed, unable to focus. Instead of spontaneously resolving as it reaches a peak, the pressure may gradually abate as the situations you are facing start to resolve.

So, in the midst of the pressure of the long haul, what's our goal? We might aspire to learn to love these periods—to not just endure but enjoy the pressure of the grind. Sometimes that's possible. Often, however, it's not realistic. When pressure is visited upon us for a long period of time, it can be profoundly uncomfortable and unenjoyable, regardless of how we approach it. Yet it is possible to not just endure these periods but actually become committed to navigating them, to see them as meaningful challenges we can rise to, and, ultimately, to emerge with the satisfaction that we were equal to the challenge. We may not wish to repeat the test, but deep down we can feel a sense of pride in our resilience, confidence that we can handle whatever life throws at us, and a feeling that we are better or stronger than we were before.

"It was bigger than rowing for me. It was about my will—it was a test of my will," said Brown as we sat in a hotel in Calgary six years later. He was in the midst of embracing another pressure-filled journey—this time setting his sights on becoming a world-class professional speaker. I had just watched him bring a room of 200 business executives to their feet, marveling at what he had endured and accomplished in just three years. "I knew if I can do this, I can do anything. And because I went all-in with my chips, the price of not seeing it through would have been too great for me. I would feel tremendous regret."

In short, the long haul may not be enjoyable, but with the right tools it can be meaningful and developmental. Our ability to look back on periods of great pressure free from regret and with admiration for ourselves is a hallmark of a life well lived and a vital source of the healthy self-esteem that leads to deep-seated satisfaction and contentment.

PEAK PRESSURE MOMENTS

A peak pressure moment is just that: a moment. It could be a footrace lasting 10 seconds or a professional exam lasting several hours, but it has a beginning and—more importantly—a well-defined conclusion with a clear range of outcomes. You pass the exam, or you don't. You hit your time in the race, or you don't. The sales pitch is successful, or it's not.

Brown's peak pressure moment arrived at the 2012 Olympic Games. His unlikely gambit had paid off: three bloody, backbreaking years after taking his first stroke he was heading to London in the men's eight boat. Just like that, the long haul was over and it was performance time. Out of the frying pan and into the fire.

The top eight teams in the world qualify for the Olympics. At the Olympics, they are divided into two heats of four. The winner of each heat automatically advances to the finals, while the remaining six boats race in what is known as a repechage, or "rep." Of the six boats in the rep, the top four join the winners of the heats in a six-boat final for all the marbles.

Canada came into the Games ranked third in the world and full of confidence. They had set a new world record at the World Cup in Lucerne three months before the Games. They knew they could win it all.

And they promptly finished dead last in their heat. Bursting with nervous energy, they delivered a season-worst time, limping in a full 12 seconds after the winners—an absolute eternity in rowing. "People were already leaving the grandstands to use the washroom before the next race," Brown remembers. "I was never more mortified in my life."

When I asked Brown about the most pressure he had ever been under, this was the period he chose—between bombing in the heat and competing in the Olympic final three days later. Following an almost unimaginable result in the heat, Brown descended into "a tornado of thinking," he recalls. "You want to be fired up, and you want to come back and show the world what you're all about. But no, I felt small. I felt like it was going to be very difficult to right the ship." He found himself watching civilians in the Olympic Village and dreaming of an escape—how comforting it would be to simply be living a normal life, laughing over dinner and watching the events on TV. He contemplated how it could have all gone wrong after the pain and suffering the team had gone through, how thoroughly they had prepared. He considered what he would do if they repeated their poor performance in the rep and failed to qualify for the finals, a plan that involved disappearing to Portugal and living out a quiet, unremarkable life.

His coach did nothing to alleviate the pressure. As the team headed into their boat at the rep, he looked at Brown and said, "Think about your son, Jeremiah. He doesn't want his dad to let him down, does he?" With a bolt of searing anger at Spracklen for putting this additional weight on him, Brown pushed off with his boat. The coxswain, who acts as a coach in the water, ultimately set things right: "It's up to the nine guys in this boat right now. We're going to do it for each other—no one else."

And they did. Rebounding from their brutal result in the heat, they rowed to a second-place finish in the rep, crossing the line half a second behind Great Britain. The immense pressure of imminent failure was off, and the pressure of the upcoming final began to build. For Brown, the waiting was excruciating: "It's fatiguing even thinking about the moments leading up to the race. The fatigue would often set in for me 48 hours before. Sweaty palms, elevated heart rate, shallow breathing. All those things would strike me so early, so I have so many memories of the fatigue, of expectation, and the foreshadowing of the pain to come. I think we all have levels of resilience and endurance, and I was at my limit a lot of that time."

Swimming in adrenaline and cortisol, Brown endured the minutiae of the final approach minute by minute—sharing silent elevator rides down to the dining hall with teammates, forcing himself to chew and swallow food with no appetite, and trying to imagine the same crushing pressure bearing down on his opponents, wondering how they would endure and taking some cold comfort in suspecting that they might not.

And then the moment arrived. Six boats lined up. Six final minutes of pain to get a verdict on whether all of the suffering had been worth it. The perfect race would require "a water rescue and eight stretchers at the finish line," Spracklen had once said. Every man in the boat knew that was what was required: maximal pain, maximal effort. The starting gun sounded and the referendum began. At 500 meters they were in third place—hundredths of a second ahead of the Netherlands. They kept pounding until the coxswain yelled, "Two minutes to go here, boys!" with a quarter boat-length separating them from Germany and Great Britain. Then there were 250 meters left—around 30 strokes. With 10 shuddering, powerful bursts they overtook the Brits and by sheer force of will held on for the next 20 strokes. Silver for Canada. A glorious end to a remarkable journey.

Peak pressure moments are different from the long haul. When they end, so does the pressure. There is no long tail-off. For Brown, the pressure was immediately replaced by ecstasy, but that's not always the case. Some peak pressure moments don't go our way and the pressure is replaced by sadness, anger, or grief. But either way, it's no longer pressure.

In peak pressure moments, the goal is simple: perform. Get out everything you are capable of when you need it most. In sport, this is known as "performance on demand." While over the long haul we define success as building confidence and the satisfaction of facing life's challenges head-on, when it comes to peak pressure moments, success is about what you get out. It is not necessarily about winning or losing—in many cases that's out of our control; it is, however, about performing to the peak of your abilities instead of shrinking from the moment.

While some peak pressure moments come on us without warning, most consist of two distinct phases: the pressure of anticipation and the pressure of performance. Almost without exception, high performers will tell you that the pressure of anticipation is worse than the pressure of performance. "Waiting is a disease," Brown wrote. As a result, while you can apply them at any time, many of the techniques we'll cover when talking about peak pressure moments are of highest value in the immediate *anticipation* of performance. This period—whether it's the 10 seconds we have to steady ourselves as a patient requiring a lifesaving intervention moves from the ambulance to the ER bay, or the week before a big presentation— is the space in which we have the most opportunity to impact our eventual mental state during the performance itself. In most peak pressure moments, managing anticipation is managing pressure.

BEING AMBIDEXTROUS

The things that make us good at navigating the long haul aren't the same as those that make us good at nailing our peak pressure moments. Some people can sustain performance through the long haul but struggle in a crisis, and a lot of elite athletes and navy SEALs who are tuned up for performance on demand don't have the most well-ordered or high-performing lives outside of their peak pressure moments.

If you can learn to be better at both performing in peak pressure moments *and* approaching the long haul with a sense of challenge, commitment, and motivation, you can become unstoppable. People who are "pressure ambidextrous" are set up to embrace the challenges that make for a rich, meaningful, and ultimately successful life.

Becoming ambidextrous is all about returning to the root causes of pressure: importance, uncertainty, and volume. While these manifest quite differently over the long haul and in peak pressure moments, the same three fundamental forces are at play—and by dealing with each of them in turn, we can transform our experience of pressure.

THE POWER OF PRESSURE MODEL

Having a mental model to turn to under pressure is vital. As we learned in Chapter 2, when we are activated our attentional focus narrows and our capacity for both higher-order thinking and absorbing new information is diminished. In these moments, simplicity is key. That is why emergency responders have the ABC framework, for airway, breathing, and circulation. It's a straightforward way to keep them focused on what matters when attention is at a premium.

In service of simplicity, I've distilled the insights on importance, uncertainty, and volume gathered across all of my research into a straightforward set of tactics—one set for the long haul and one set for peak pressure moments. Each of the six chapters in Part 2 discusses one facet of the following model:

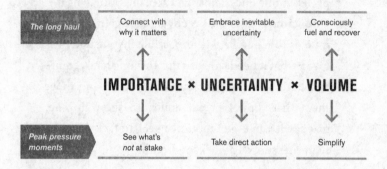

When it comes to success over the long haul, we will examine three core imperatives:

1. **Connect with why it matters:** Over the long haul, navigating importance is about creating a clear line of sight from the day-to-day grind to what matters most to you. It's about keeping importance front and center in the midst of all of the ups and downs that accompany any busy life. When our daily decisions become disconnected from what matters to us for too long, it is hard to sustain a sense of commitment to the journey.

2. **Embrace inevitable uncertainty:** High performers adopt a mindset over the long haul that embraces the uncertainty inherent in our lives. This mindset consists of an often challenging combination of accepting that there are things we cannot control (and that therefore may not go our way) while at the same time holding a sense of optimism about the future. It is a belief that if

we focus on our own actions, everything will work out as it should. Optimism is the difference between simply accepting uncertainty and actually embracing it.

3. **Consciously fuel and recover:** Navigating the volume of the long haul is impossible if your body isn't given what it needs to keep up. The long haul requires sufficient sleep and an approach to food and movement that supports your ability to show up energized, with an even emotional keel, to tackle another high-pressure day, week, or month.

For peak pressure moments, our three core tools are:

1. **See what's *not* at stake:** In peak pressure moments we often give the stakes too much weight. Consciously or unconsciously, we focus on everything we have to win or lose, and lose sight of what won't change regardless of the outcome. Learning to see the entire picture—both what's at stake and what *isn't* at stake—is vital to regulating emotion and performing well in peak pressure moments.

2. **Take direct action:** Direct action is our biggest ally when it comes to taming uncertainty. Identifying what we can control and then focusing on making progress (however small) is the surest antidote to uncertainty under pressure. This requires first separating out what you can control (your behavior and mindset) from what you can't (other people and outcomes). In many ways, direct action is the central skill in navigating peak pressure.

3. **Simplify:** One of the great derailers of performance is distraction. When it comes to volume in our peak pressure moments, the imperative is quite straightforward: eliminate it. Put aside anything that isn't directly related to performance so that your focus can be complete and total. Of course, that is easier said than done—as we will see.

THE SPACE BETWEEN TRIGGER AND RESPONSE

There is one fundamental thing that applies to both the long haul and peak pressure moments: the ability to put space between trigger and response. To notice what you are feeling, thinking, and experiencing physically before you move to action. No one ability is more fundamental to being pressure ambidextrous than expanding that space. It is a precondition to accessing all of the tactics we'll explore in the coming chapters.

My mom, an amazing woman with a double master's degree in adult education and counseling psychology and a long career as a counselor to elite athletes of every stripe, illustrates this with a very different ABC process than the one emergency responders use. In every situation, there is a point A that represents what you think and feel, and a point C that represents what you do—the behavior that others see. Most of us jump straight from point A to point C: we think or feel something that immediately drives our behavior. Under pressure, we want to remember that there is a point B—the moment between A and C when you can observe and choose how you want to be. The more we can become conscious of and expand the length of point B, the more productive our responses are likely to be.

When we are under immense pressure, we often lose sight of our capacity for free will. When importance and uncertainty strike, we become our pounding heart, we become our anger or anxiety, we become our racing minds. And when we become these things, we are no longer in the driver's seat. Our anxiety is driving. Our untamed thoughts are driving. The primitive brain has the wheel and we lose the space between stimulus and response—we simply react.

Central to managing pressure is realizing that we are not our thoughts, we are not our feelings, and we are not our bodies. These are our tools of action in the world, but they don't define who we are or what we are capable of. What does this mean? Well, as far as we know, human beings are the only creatures on Earth who have the capacity to step back and observe ourselves. We can think about what we are thinking about. We can notice how we're feeling. We can observe what's happening to our body, our heart rate, our breathing. Other animals don't have this ability. When a snake is slithering through the undergrowth and hears a twig snap, it doesn't pause to think, *Huh, I'm really anxious right now. My back is really arched*—it just attacks. It's a hardwired pattern of stimulus → response.

Human beings, however, have another gear. We have the part of us that notices when we're unable to stop thinking about events of the day as we are trying to fall asleep and searches for ways to help us relax, and we have that internal voice that says *Okay, calm down—take a breath* when we see another child give our kid a shove on the playground and we are ready to pounce. The part of us that observes our thoughts, coaches our actions, and soothes our feelings is what we call the "self"—who we truly are.

The self can hold all of who we are—currently and potentially. It is the source of our inner wisdom. The self is like the conductor in an orchestra: it hears the music in its purest form, our best self, and then tries to coax it out of the orchestra of our feelings, thoughts, and sensations. Under pressure, our ability to move to the position of impartial observer, notice the impact pressure is having on us, and then choose or coach our response is what makes us truly free. There is a big difference between *being* angry and *noticing* I'm angry. When I *am* angry, I become my anger—I lash out. When I *notice* I'm angry, I can connect with my capacity to choose, engage my free will, and decide how I want to respond.

Many would call this position of observation "mindfulness." At Third Factor, we call it "active awareness"—that is, I become actively aware of the impact that pressure is having on me and I *choose* what I am going to do.

This ability to step back is the foundation of being pressure ambidextrous. It is the prerequisite to success both under peak pressure and over the long haul. On top of this foundation, however, very different choices are required for success in peak pressure than for satisfaction over the long haul. It turns out that being good at handling pressure is two skills, not one. And nowhere is this clearer than when it comes to managing importance—which is where we will begin our journey through the pressure equation.

PART 2

HARNESSING THE POWER OF PRESSURE

CHAPTER 4

CONNECT WITH WHY IT MATTERS

IMPORTANCE OVER THE LONG HAUL

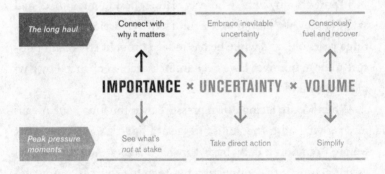

In her brilliant book *The Upside of Stress*, Stanford's Kelly McGonigal offers the following insight: "Stress and meaning are inextricably linked. You don't stress out about things you don't care about, and you can't create a meaningful life without stress." I happened to read this book at a time when my wife and I were wrestling with the decision of whether to have a third child. We both come from bigger families (I'm the youngest of four, she's the youngest of three) and envisioned a future with a "big family table" full of loud conversation and, eventually, partners and grandkids. At the same time, neither of us was particularly keen to endure the sleep-deprived pressure cooker that another baby would add to the mix.

We had been debating back and forth for several months when, reading in bed just before turning the lights out, I got hit between the eyes by three reflective questions McGonigal poses: "Is there anything you would like to do, experience, accept, or change, if only you were not afraid of the stress it might bring into your life? How would your life be enhanced by pursuing any of these possibilities? What is the cost to you of not allowing yourself to pursue them?"

I turned to my wife, who was reading beside me in bed, and said, "Honey, we should have a third kid." As I write this, Henry is three years old, and while he has indeed brought stress and pressure to bear, our lives have been immeasurably enhanced by having him around.

When we are facing down pressure over the long haul, meaning is a vital ally. The ability to clear a line of sight from what we are doing on a daily basis to what matters most to us is an essential tool. If the connection between the sources of pressure in our lives and what is important to us is blocked or unclear for long enough, the pressure we face can begin to feel relentless and debilitating.

When we observe individuals who have been able to accomplish great things in the face of sustained pressure, nearly all are driven by a strong sense of purpose. Reflecting on his long haul, Jeremiah Brown told me: "At the end, what you are left with is the answer to the question 'Why are you doing this?' And is that purpose strong enough to take you through inordinate amounts of discomfort and anxiety? Ultimately, it's about meaning."

MOMENTS OF MEANING

A lot has been written recently on meaning. Whether it's Simon Sinek's essential *Start with Why*, Bill George of Harvard's *True North*, or Dan Pontefract's *The Purpose Effect*, many of the best and brightest thinkers on leadership and human performance have turned their attention to the transformative effect that a connection with purpose can have.

In the midst of this renaissance of meaning, I think it's important for all of us to remember that purpose is not an all-encompassing thing that envelops us and provides us with constant energy. To return to my personal example, let's talk about kids. Anyone who knows me would say that my three kids are a vital source of meaning in my life. Helping them reach their potential is a huge part of why I do what I do. And 80% of the time, having young kids is a complete pain in the ass: they fight nearly constantly; our five-year-old gets ready at one speed—three-toed sloth—regardless of how late we might be; our oldest still cannot remember to use cutlery like a normal human being despite being reminded 10 times at every meal for eight straight years; car rides to my in-laws in Ottawa are five-hour ordeals that have my wife and I repeatedly questioning why they do not offer the option of a soundproof taxicab-style partition in a consumer SUV. And yet there are those moments when the meaning inherent in being a parent crystalizes. I will admit that this often occurs when the kids are asleep. Sometimes, however, it happens in the daytime. When my daughter, Stella, was around seven months old, in the early winter of 2014, we were out grocery shopping and it started to snow for the first time that year. Big, puffy snowflakes began lazily falling—almost like being inside a snow globe. Stella was a spring baby and had never seen snow before, and as I pushed her stroller out of the store, she started laughing and grabbing at the snowflakes drifting toward her. I sped up a bit and started jogging with the stroller down the sidewalk toward our house, snow flying beside us, her laughter ringing in my ears. It was magical. I had a similar feeling this past year watching our oldest, Jack, master parallel skiing. As I moved from helping him down the hill to attempting to keep up with him, I felt a deep and abiding sense of pride (which lasted until we ate lunch in the lodge and I saw him begin to eat his salad with his fingers).

In short, meaning is not a constant thing—it happens in moments. Whether it's Stella outside the grocery store or Jack on the hill, there are moments when life with all of its ups and downs intersects for a minute with what really matters to you.

Even in the midst of a long haul that is deeply meaningful and incredibly important to us, we will spend a large part of our time disconnected from meaning and working toward something less noble but equally important: achievement. Our kids need to be fed and clothed. Conflicts need to be adjudicated. We need a place to live. Our monthly expense reports need to be filed.

A satisfying long haul comes from increasing the frequency with which we have these moments of connection while on the journey of achievement. As we pursue our goals, are we regularly nourished by connecting with what matters most to us—or do we have long stretches when it feels unclear or disconnected?

MEANING ≠ HAPPINESS

There is a distinct difference between connecting with meaning and being happy. Being connected to what matters to you can be a satisfying experience (either in the moment or in retrospect) and can sometimes be accompanied by feelings of joy or happiness, but in no way does it *necessarily* make for a happy long haul.

One of the more remarkable long hauls is Rick Hansen's Man in Motion World Tour. A gifted athlete and outdoorsman from an early age, Hansen was hitchhiking home from a fishing trip in the back of a pickup truck at age 15 when the truck rolled and he sustained a spinal cord injury that paralyzed him from the waist down. After a tough recovery period, Hansen got into wheelchair racing in the late 1970s, and he dominated the sport. From 1979 to 1984 he won six medals at the Paralympic Games and 19 International Wheelchair Marathons, including three world championships. In 1983 he received the Lou Marsh Trophy for Canadian athlete of the year along with co-recipient Wayne Gretzky.

At the peak of his domination of wheelchair racing, Hansen began to toy with a seemingly absurd idea: circumnavigating the world by wheelchair. It was a vision that would require wheeling more than the equivalent of two marathons every day for 26 months. It was the long haul in every sense of the phrase.

Thirty-five years later, as we sat in Hansen's office overlooking the Fraser River in Vancouver, he marveled at the audacity of what he'd set out to do: "Out of all the pressure I'd gone through, none of it came close to the pressure I felt leading up to the launch of the Man in Motion tour. The outlandish statements that I had made: that I was going to wheel around the world, that I was going to create awareness about the potential of people with disabilities, and raise $10 million for spinal cord research, and that we were going to go through 34 countries in four continents before computers and cell phones. And you're going to do this how?"

Hansen's vision and passion for the tour had encouraged sponsors to get on board, but as the launch date receded in the face of immense logistical challenges, the pressure became relentless. "It was completely consuming. It wasn't just going out there and training for 8 to 10 hours in a day. It was putting on your suit and breaking up your training, having a quick shower, going to have a lunch with a potential sponsor, then going back out into the cold in a rainy, slimy, wet December Vancouver day, out on the sea wall in Stanley Park, and putting in your miles, and then doing it again in the afternoon, and all over again in the evening. It just seemed like it was so much."

The pressure started to affect him deeply. "I wasn't sleeping well. I also knew that I was getting crankier and crankier. I was scared. I really felt that the pressure I was under was so immense that I was going to crumble before I even started, and I was going to take down everybody around me."

But of course he didn't crumble—he persevered. On March 21, 1985, he addressed the large crowd that had gathered for a triumphant send-off that had been advertised on all of the major radio stations in town. "I'm telling all these people that I'm wheeling around the world. I'm exhausted. I had hardly slept at all that night. It's crappy weather out. It's March. It's cold. There's an iconic photo of me with the premier of the province, and Betty and Rolly Fox, Terry's mom and dad. I'm speaking. I look like a deer in the headlights, honest to God. I see the photo and I know what I was thinking. I remember it because I felt a twinge in my left shoulder." Not exactly the iconic, heartwarming send-off he had hoped for.

As he prepared to head offstage, his friend Jim Taylor came by: "He worked his way through the crowd, leaned over the chair and offered one final, encouraging word: 'Don't forget,' he said cheerfully, 'a book called *Almost Around the World in a Wheelchair* won't sell shit.'"

"That literally was the greatest accomplishment of the Man in Motion World Tour, that first day, taking the first step," recalls Hansen. The first day itself wasn't exactly smooth sailing: the support van crashed into the first overpass it encountered, demolishing the spare wheelchair that had been strapped to the roof in a crate. But they were underway.

When he reflects on how he managed to make it to that first day, Hansen doesn't mince words: "I had lived the experience of humiliation, of being handicapped—not by my injury but by society, by people, by the physical and attitudinal barriers I encountered. I really did want to use some of my precious life energy and talent to make a difference. I came to realize that there was only one hope—and that was that I had to just be all-in, almost like it was for my survival. I put it all on the line."

With a clear line of sight to the meaning of the pressure he was enduring, Hansen accomplished the unthinkable, wheeling over 24,000 miles across 34 countries in the course of 26 months. "It was just one stroke at a time, one day at a time, visualizing the outcome that you think will happen, and trying to reconcile the incredible gap between the dream and reality," he says. "The despair of that, and the frustration of that, and sometimes the anger, and the bitterness of that, and yet to know that what you're doing is not chasing a fantasy or an illusion, but something that is manifesting each day, and to honor that, and to try to find a way to celebrate that."

Hansen's words clearly convey what "connecting to meaning" sounds like at its deepest level. And you may note that it sounds nothing like happiness. In describing his journey, Hansen regularly uses words like "despair," "anger," and "scared"—how it felt like he might "crumble"—and this is before even getting into the actual tour itself. Connecting with meaning is a vital ingredient to the long haul, and at the same time it often brings even more suffering in the moment simply because it prolongs your ability to endure.

Before we shut the door on meaning and happiness, there is one very important caveat: how happy we are in the midst of an experience and how happy we are when looking back on that experience in the future are two very different things.

In *The Power of Moments*, a terrific book about designing moments that delight, authors Chip and Dan Heath share an experiment in which participants are subjected to a standard pain tolerance test that involves submerging their hands into uncomfortably cold water (57 degrees Fahrenheit—try it for yourself sometime). The first test lasts for 60 seconds. The second begins with the same 60-second submersion and then continues an additional 30 seconds in which the water is warmed slightly, to 59 degrees. Without knowing how long each test lasted, participants are asked which one they would like to repeat for the third round. It's a seemingly obviously choice: take the 60-second version. In the second iteration, you still have the same 60 seconds of suffering *and* you get an additional 30 seconds of discomfort. And yet 69% of subjects chose the longer test. This seemingly irrational result can be explained by what is known as the peak-end effect, which has demonstrated that, when looking back on experiences, people tend to evaluate them based not on an overall average level of happiness, but rather on the *peak* (either high or low) and the *end* of the experience. In this experiment, both tests had the same peak, but the *end* of the second version was more pleasant, and so it was the one that most people chose to repeat.

The implications of the peak-end effect for the long haul are profound. Based on Hansen's recounting of the Man in Motion tour, if you had surveyed him hour to hour and asked about his level of happiness, it's highly likely you would have received a lot of low marks. Thousands of hours were marked by illness, headwinds, mechanical difficulties, pressure sores, and, in the case of a particularly low period in the United States, a complete absence of local support that made him feel like he was having no impact whatsoever. And yet the end of his tour was remarkable: Hansen raised over $36 million for spinal cord research, far exceeding his goal of $10 million, and returned to a hero's welcome in a packed 50,000-seat stadium in his hometown. Had he not had the connection to meaning that allowed him to persevere through all those brutal, painful hours, the end of the experience would have been quite different, marked not by accomplishment and jubilation, but by regret and disappointment. An hour-by-hour accounting of the journey would be similar, but his memory of the overall experience would be profoundly different.

In short, connecting to meaning may prolong suffering in the short term, but it minimizes regret over the long haul. When the memories of the hour-to-hour grind fade, the satisfaction of having done something important are permanently etched. For my wife and me, our memories of the sleep-deprived first four months with Henry are already long gone, replaced by a series of peaks that make it all worth it.

HOW DO YOU FIND MEANING?

So where does meaning come from? The answer to that is ultimately very personal. What provides one person with a sense of purpose can be profoundly uninteresting to another. I once met someone whose mission in life was to eradicate peanuts from sports stadiums. It mattered greatly to her, as the mother of a son with a nut allergy, but it wasn't something that would sustain me over the long haul—I love the crunch of peanut shells under my seat in the middle of a baseball game.

At the same time, there are three fundamental ways in which we derive meaning: *growth, contribution,* and *connection.*

GROWTH

In many ways, the US Naval Academy at Annapolis is a perfect microcosm for studying pressure. Deliberately designed to push people to their physical and mental limits, the academy's freshman-year basic training is a crucible. For Shaun Francis, chair and chief executive officer of wellness company Medcan, the experience was like nothing he had ever experienced. Rules dictate every aspect of a first-year's life. Your head is shaved. You're required to run everywhere you go, and in a certain high-knees style. You must not move your head when walking, and must travel parallel to the path and turn only at intersections. You're allowed to chew your food only three times. "It's designed to create a very high-pressure environment because you'll be leading in a high-pressure world," says Francis.

Sounds intense, right? Yet Francis, like thousands before and since, remembers this period of immense pressure as a hugely formative period: "It gave you confidence that you could accomplish almost anything." After the naval academy, Francis took on another high-pressure assignment, at an investment bank in New York. The pay was great, and the pressure-cooker environment was similar to that in Annapolis, but he quickly burned out and quit. So what was the difference? Why was one pressure-cooker experience not only tolerable but actually satisfying, while the other couldn't end quickly enough? It certainly wasn't Francis's time-management capabilities. Nor did the financial rewards have much impact. At the end of the day, it came back to a simple question:

IS THIS PRESSURE HELPING ME GROW?

"The Naval Academy is a developmental experience. It's designed to keep you in the navy, not get rid of you," recalls Francis. "It's designed to create an officer, a leader for a combat situation. Whereas at the investment bank, it wasn't a priority to develop you. That was up to you. They pay everyone enough money—and they have enough smart people that will make it to the top jobs—so they don't really care."

One of my favorite (and, in my opinion, criminally under-rated) books is *The Progress Principle* by Teresa Amabile and Steven Kramer. Amabile and Kramer, two professors at Harvard Business School, were in search of a better understanding of what factors led to what they called a "positive inner work life." They defined "inner work life" as a combination of three things: how people were *thinking* about their daily work, how people were *feeling* in their daily work, and how much *motivation* people felt to get work done. People with a positive inner work life were those who had positive thoughts about their work (their colleagues, the organization, and so on), moved through the day with an overall positive mood, and ultimately felt a strong drive to accomplish their work. People with a negative inner work life were those who held negative thoughts, feelings, and drive.

Now, of course, inner work life is a state, not a personality trait. All of us have days when we are more positive or more negative in our thoughts, feelings, and motivation. In order to determine what tipped the balance on a day-by-day basis, Amabile and Kramer devised a massive research project, recruiting 238 people in 26 project teams across seven companies in three industries. For approximately four months, each of these 238 individuals submitted a diary form at the end of every work-day. In the form they were asked to rate their inner work life—thoughts, emotions, drive—that day using numerical scales, and then they were asked this vital question: "Briefly describe one event from today that stands out in your mind." The effort resulted in an inside look at almost 12,000 days of work—a massive trove of data.

As Amabile and Kramer crunched the data, an elegantly simple conclusion began to emerge: "Of all the positive events that influence inner work life, the single most powerful is progress in meaningful work." On days when people had made progress, they felt positive and motivated; on days when they had experienced setbacks or inhibitors to their work, their inner work life suffered.

When we think back on periods during which we were under tremendous pressure, the ones that tend to seem most meaningful and important to us are those in which we felt like we were growing. Simply put: *growth gives meaning to pressure*. If I believe the pressure is helping me improve in a way that matters to me, that can provide a tremendous source of meaning that can transform my experience.

CONTRIBUTION

The second major source of meaning in high-pressure situations is contribution. For Rick Hansen, enduring the long haul of the Man in Motion World Tour was about contributing to the creation of a world without barriers. He wanted to bring hope to millions of people with disabilities—to show them that anything was possible.

Most of the longer periods of pressure we endure don't have nearly as clear a line of sight to contribution as Hansen's, but the same core principle remains. When I feel like I am helping others, my own journey becomes more meaningful and satisfying. Biological imperatives aside, this is at the heart of the decision to have and raise children. It's a stressful and often unrewarding undertaking, but it is deeply rooted in the meaning provided by contribution.

The core question that gets us in touch with contribution is:

WILL ENDURING THIS PRESSURE HELP OTHERS?

When I was a kid, there was one certainty in life: on Sunday night, my dad's travel agent would knock on the door of our house and deliver a stack of plane tickets for the coming week. Sometimes she would come in to briefly discuss the coming week's plans; other times the tickets would simply get pushed through the mail slot and land with a thump. But they were always there. My father, Peter Jensen, is an amazing man who has a PhD in sport psychology, has attended 10 Olympic Games as a member of Team Canada, and pioneered the application of coaching principles in the business world. At that time, he was on the road constantly, delivering over 150 workshops and presentations a year across the globe. Later in life, he would receive a beautiful model airplane in a carved wooden box from Air Canada as a thank you for a lifetime of regular travel.

Much later, when I made the decision to follow in my dad's footsteps and strike out on a career as a speaker, we had a chance to talk about what the job is like. Obviously, it's a privilege to have people want to hear what you have to say. And yet, when you're at an airport convention center, about to deliver the same speech for the 40th time in as many days and missing your family, the routine can start to feel a little bit relentless. My father's advice was straightforward: "No matter how many times I deliver the same presentation, no matter how boring it is to hear myself say the same words again, I look out at the audience and find someone who is really interested—nodding, leaning in. And I remind myself that this person can really benefit from this stuff. And that I owe it to them to be engaged and interested."

When we connect to contribution, even if it's as simple as what value we can bring to one person, it can transform our experience of pressure.

CONNECTION

Finally, we have the meaning that comes from growing closer to others. When I ask people in workshops or speeches to talk about a "moment of meaning" they have had in the past 30 days, this theme is inevitably the one that dominates: time with their families, reconnecting with friends, or a meaningful connection with somebody new.

In February 2013, a year after winning a gold medal in trampoline at the London Olympics, Rosie MacLennan had a bad fall while snowboarding and suffered a concussion. She had had a concussion once before, and it hadn't impacted her performance significantly, so beyond the typical recovery, she didn't give it much attention. Plus, she had also hurt her ankle and was focused on rehabbing that joint, which is particularly vital to jumping. Once the ankle was recovered and she started jumping in June, however, she realized something was off. "I started getting lost in the air," she recalls. When you're launching yourself 25 feet high and performing multiple rotations on three axes, this is a terrifying problem. "When you lose yourself, you feel like a ragdoll, kind of uncontrollably flipping through the air. And I got really, really scared of a certain group of basic skills that I had been doing for years." Driven by the determination and discipline of an elite athlete, MacLennan tried to will herself through the fear and disorientation. It didn't work. "I fell in training and got another concussion." Still, she persevered, managing to compete at the Pan American Games in her hometown of Toronto in the summer of 2015. Soon after that, with only a year to go before the Olympics in Rio de Janeiro, "I got hit in the head again—and that's when things really started to spiral out of control symptom-wise. It was really bad," she says.

MacLennan visited specialists across North America. Unable to train, all she could do was focus on her health. With the World Championships—the key qualifying event for the Olympics—approaching, she hadn't been on a trampoline in months. Finally, she was able to start jumping just four weeks prior to competition, and the first run-through of her competition routine, after four and a half months off, took place four days before her departure. As she continued to push herself to the limit, she crashed again the day before she left.

Finally, she agreed to do an easier routine at the World Championships. "I think the most pressure was when I was trying to push myself to do these routines that I just clearly wasn't ready to do mentally, physically. And then when we changed it to a routine that I had more confidence in, that alleviated a lot of the pressure and allowed me to then focus on the performance." Going in with a very different goal than at previous World Championships, where she wanted to dominate, she did what she needed to do and qualified for the 2016 Olympic Games in Rio—a remarkable feat with almost no preparation.

With this odyssey as a backdrop, MacLennan made her way to Rio as the defending gold medalist, with all of the attendant pressure that comes from being the champion looking to repeat. At the Olympics, the competitors get only one day of training in the venue itself, the day before they compete. And in the midst of all of the madness, she had a moment of connection: "I was on the trampoline with one of the competitors from China, who was favored to win. And we were just having such a good time. We were chatting and cheering each other on and smiling. And I remember looking around and seeing other people who were stressed and anxious and—I don't know—I just thought back to that moment after my injury where I was thinking *I just want to jump on the trampoline* and not thinking I was going to get my chance."

For MacLennan, this moment of connection made it all worthwhile: "I was just so grateful for that moment and filled with so much joy. Competing the next day was stressful, but I felt very comfortable because I knew the feeling that I had the day before was my gold medal. That was the pinnacle."

Having already won her own internal gold medal, she went out there and won the actual gold medal for good measure too, becoming a two-time Olympic champion.

CLEARING A LINE OF SIGHT TO MEANING

So, practically speaking, how do we ensure that we stay connected to what matters when we're under long-term pressure? Ultimately, we need to clear a line of sight to meaning in a way that is authentic and not forced, and that positions meaning appropriately within the context of achievement—recognizing that we need to optimize for both meaning and achievement. To do that, let's bring into play a process that was first introduced in my father's 1991 book *The Inside Edge* and has been refined over the past 30 years of our work on resilience under pressure. We are at our most resilient over the long haul when we see how our daily decisions add up to achieving goals that are in service of a vision for our future that is rooted in what matters most to us—our North Star. The following diagram is a map to how these four components—daily decisions, goals, vision, and North Star—work together to help clarify our line of sight to what is important.

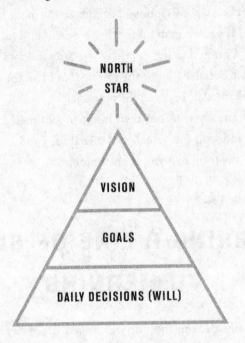

Let's examine each of these elements in turn.

- **North Star** is the meaning that motivates and guides us. Your North Star is what matters most to you in terms of your own growth and your contribution and connection to others.
- **Vision** is a clear and compelling mental image of the future. If meaning is ethereal, vision is practical. A solid vision is like a postcard from "future you" describing what life is like at some point down the road.

- **Goals** are the things you need to accomplish, learn, acquire, or let go of in order to move toward your vision.
- **Daily decisions** are where the rubber hits the road. These are the 100 small moments every day that ultimately determine whether you are moving toward your goals or away from them.

Under the pressure of the long haul, being able to clearly articulate your version of this map can pay huge dividends. If you are in a position to choose your pressure, the map can act as a planning tool to channel meaning into action. Rick Hansen was very clear from the start on his North Star—creating a world without barriers for disabled people—which he then translated into the vision of a tour around the world. Implementing that vision involved some very ambitious goals around fundraising, personal training, assembling a team, etcetera, and those goals drove his daily decisions—decisions that, as we saw earlier, were often difficult and would have been almost impossible to stick to without a compelling sense of his North Star and vision.

Most of the time you don't get to choose your pressures, however, so your North Star may be less clear. Let's imagine you are facing down months of tremendous personal uncertainty that is out of your control. Perhaps your company has been acquired and has announced a restructuring that will see your team merged with one from the parent company. This will result in layoffs as the two teams are brought together, but they aren't yet clear on what form the layoffs will take or when exactly they will occur—"sometime in the next six months" is the water cooler chatter. That six months has the potential to be characterized by a complete disconnect between your daily decisions and what's important to you. As you go through the motions of doing your job, your mind will be elsewhere, your conversations with colleagues and family will center on what you'll do if your job gets cut, and you'll feel disengaged from work. In short, it will be a period of purgatory to be endured.

But let's look at how you could choose to see the situation as meaningful and important—and in doing so change your experience. Figure 3 shows how it could look if you take the time to work through your North Star, vision, and goals for the period.

Taking the time to articulate the situation in this way, to step back from fighting the daily fires to get a sense of how you can grow, contribute, and connect, and what success will look like—warts and all—can help you tap into a deeper source of energy and approach the situation with an entirely different perspective. Now, is the six months likely to be enjoyable? No! No one likes operating under immense uncertainty around their employment. Remember that our goal for the long haul isn't necessarily to make it fun, but rather to emerge from it with a sense of satisfaction that we have risen to the challenge, and with no regrets about how we chose to proceed. Connecting with importance gives us the best shot at doing just that.

NORTH STAR	**Growth:** *How is this pressure helping me grow?* I will be confident in my ability to handle anything, and it will increase my ability to operate under uncertainty, which is a dominant feature of the modern work world. **Contribution:** *Will enduring this pressure help others?* Yes. If I show up engaged and energized on a daily basis, I can positively impact my team's experience through a difficult period. **Connection:** *Will this pressure bring me closer to those I care about?* If handled appropriately, yes, it could strengthen the bonds I have with my colleagues who are going through the same experience.
VISION	*What will it look like six months from now if I have risen to this challenge?* I will have maintained my health, be seen as a competent and strong leader by my team, have stayed engaged with my partners and kids, and have strong references from others in the business. Further, I will have a clear sense of my options for the future and will have strengthened my technical skills to stay relevant. Hopefully, I will also still have my job but that may be out of my control.
GOALS	*What do I need to accomplish, learn, acquire, or let go of to achieve my vision?* I must continue to accomplish the core tasks of my job, take a more active role in strategic planning for the department, learn technology skills that I've let lapse, and let go of my need to control the outcome.

FIGURE 3: *North Star, vision, and goals.*

WHEN IMPORTANCE
IS ELUSIVE

Jeff Dionne had just changed roles; following a boss he respected, he had moved from the clinical side of the house at St. Joseph's Health Centre in Toronto to a newly formed organizational development (OD) group. As part of their mandate, a few months after Dionne joined, this group was tasked with conducting the hospital's first-ever engagement survey, assessing how motivated and committed to their work the hospital employees felt. In his role as director of leadership and organizational development, he was made the point person. Now, fielding the first-ever engagement survey in a large organization is no small task—it requires a coordinated effort across all sectors of the organization to drive high levels of completion, report the results, and then ensure that the outcomes from the survey get translated into action. To try to keep costs down, Dionne's OD group had agreed to pull together all of the reporting on the survey in-house. As a result, they had to produce more than 215 individual reports—one for every team of more than five people in the organization—including presentations, heat maps, and other data for the team's manager. And given that this was the group's first major project, there was a lot at stake for their credibility in the organization.

The survey was fielded in February, and the team was on the hook to deliver all 215 reports by June. Then, shortly after the survey closed in May, the hospital announced a clinical restructuring. All 215 teams were reshuffled, and the human resources team's data on who was where became hopelessly mixed up. "All of the data that had come through in February in our HR information system now had to be reorganized to align with the new directors and managers," Dionne remembers. "We couldn't trust the data—for example, someone would report to a Joe Smith and someone would report to a Joseph Smith. And they'd be mixed up." These mix-ups resulted in several highly stressful presentations to senior leadership in which inaccuracies in the data would come to light that hadn't been caught in time. "They said to us, 'You better make damn sure this is good information—because we already don't believe its validity.' So, you then had to go back and verify to make sure that all of the filtering of that was correct and make sure that all of the names of the departments were still matching. It was very, very stressful, and hectic at the time."

It all came to a head when Dionne found himself alone at the office at 11:35 p.m. on a Friday night, working on a heat map for a presentation to the hospital's chief financial officer. "I remember running down to the library—because that's where we had our color printer—to grab this 11- by 17-inch printout, which had a big color-coded heat map on it, and looking up at the clock and seeing that it was 11:35. I said to myself, *What am I doing?* I was doing this for a person I respected, but I was like, *What is this doing to me?*" With two young kids at home, the trade-offs started to weigh on him. "At this point, my daughter's 7, my son is 11. I've got to get up the next morning to then get them to their Saturday morning activities." He was burning the midnight oil, exhausted constantly, and emotionally flat.

It's easy to connect to meaning when you're on a global journey to eradicate barriers for people with disabilities, like Rick Hansen. It's much more difficult when you're standing alone at the office printer close to midnight on a Friday night crunching data for an engagement survey. But for most of us, Dionne's story is closer to our day-to-day reality than Hansen's.

Dionne made it through his long haul. He worked with the team to reorganize their workflow, centralizing all report production with one person and, thanks to his epiphany at the printer, trying to mitigate as much as possible the impact on work–life balance. Several years later, he's now in his old boss's role and the engagement survey has become an annual event—highly successful and close to routine. So what allowed him to make it through? "I've never had the crisis of meaning at St. Joe's. I've never lost my why. My old boss said to me, 'You know we always say that we put our patients first, but I would disagree with that. We should be putting our patients second. We should be putting the people who put those patients first, first.' That's what OD does. It allows us to build our people in the organization, our physicians, our staff, our leaders. And for me, having been at this organization for so long—you know, my kids were born here, my dad's been a cancer patient here, my sister as a physician has been treated here. I've always had that meaning and connection here. This has been my purpose, so I never lost that."

That doesn't mean there aren't long, dark nights. "Sometimes I'm like, *Oh my gosh, is this ever going to end?*" Dionne says. "But I didn't lose the drive, because I knew it was the right thing to do."

Even in the mundane, we can connect with contribution and growth. At the same time, if we have to search too hard to answer our questions about meaning, if it becomes difficult to see how the pressure in our lives is connected to growth, contribution, or connection, then we need to think about the pressure we are taking on. It's fine to have a hazy view from daily decisions to meaning for periods of time. But if you can't answer those questions for too long, it may be time to reevaluate.

Often, however, the answer is simply to make sure we are noticing, and even savoring, our moments of meaning instead of letting them slip quietly by. Pause to take pride in the ways you are growing. Notice the contributions you are making and allow yourself to feel satisfied. Hold on to the moments when you look around the table or the room and feel, for a fleeting moment, a deep sense of connection. These are the moments that sustain us through the inevitable ups and downs of the long haul—they are precious, and they must be cultivated.

CHAPTER 5

SEE WHAT'S *NOT* AT STAKE

IMPORTANCE IN PEAK PRESSURE MOMENTS

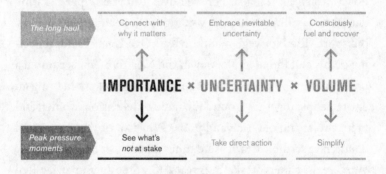

t was early February 1994, two weeks before the start of the XVII Olympic Winter Games, and the Norwegian long-track speed skater Johann Olav Koss was hiding in a hotel stairwell, crying his eyes out. At that moment, Koss was considered the best in the world at his event. He had won two medals at the 1992 Olympics in Albertville, a gold in the 1,500 meters and a silver in the 10,000, and he was the reigning World Cup champion in the 5,000/10,000-meter class.

But in two weeks, he would tackle something new: an Olympics in his home country of Norway, where speed skating amounts to a national obsession. Heading into the Olympics, Koss was carrying a nation's hopes on his back. The pressure was compounded by the fact that he was competing in an individual event. He didn't have teammates to share his burden.

It can be hard for people in North America to grasp the popularity of speed skating in countries like Norway and the Netherlands. In Norway, Koss had the sort of celebrity reserved for the top tier of society, the recipient of adulation given in North America only to a select group of professional athletes—think basketball's LeBron James in the United States, or hockey's Connor McDavid in Canada. For well over 100 years, speed skating has sat alongside cross-country skiing as the beating heart of Nordic sport. The Norwegian author Karl Ove Knausgaard, reflecting on his childhood in Norway in the *New York Times*, painted a clear picture: "What is it about speedskating that could bring an entire people together around the radio or television, women and men, young and old, rich and poor? What was it that compelled children to scribble down skate times and collect them in books? Why are the names of [skating greats] Kay Stenshjemmet, Jan Egil Storholt, Sten Stensen and Amund Sjøbrend etched in my memory 40 years after they hung up their skates for good, whereas I have long since forgotten the names of prominent politicians of the day or the teachers I had at school?"

When Lillehammer won the bid for the 1994 Games in 1988, Koss was already an elite athlete. He would win the overall World Cup for the 1,500-meter in the 1989–1990 season for the first time, then stay at the top for six straight years. In Lillehammer he would be competing in three races: the 1,500-meter, the 5,000-meter, and the 10,000-meter. Koss was the favorite in all three distances. The Norwegians expected him to bring home three gold medals, cementing the country's dominance in the sport.

Koss, however, was not so sure: "A few weeks before the Olympics, I had the worst race of my life," he remembers. At the World Cup immediately before the Olympics he gave a rare lackluster performance, placing eighth. In an event that often sees photo finishes, Koss's time was 17 seconds behind the best Dutch skaters. "I felt like I couldn't skate anymore," he recalled. "I had lost the feeling, the emotion of skating. I lost the technique."

There was *physical* strain, too. The media fixated on Koss's nagging knee soreness. He was having problems with his skates, believing that the position of the blade was off-center from his foot. "So I was dealing with equipment failure, physical failure, and technical failure," he recalls. Some in the media questioned whether the man known as "King Koss" could win at the Olympics: "Oh, he's not good enough anymore," they said. "He can't stand up to the pressure."

This toxic brew of uncertainty—around his equipment, his health, and his capability—would have been enough on its own, but what made the pressure almost unbearable was the *national* importance of his event, the awareness that the Norwegian national identity would suffer if he failed to do anything but win a gold medal. "You felt you had the whole country on your shoulders," Koss says.

On February 8, with less than a week to go before his first Olympic race on February 14, the pressure climaxed: "I really felt like I did not have everything ready," Koss says. "My fear of failure was astronomical . . . I felt like failure [at the Olympics] would create failure for the rest of my life."

All of which led to a remarkable scene: one of the greatest athletes in the world, on the eve of the biggest competition of his life, crying at the bottom of a staircase in his hotel. Koss considered quitting. The pressure seemed too much.

Thankfully, Koss happened to be with his sport psychologist at the time of his breakdown. "I was bawling my eyes out," Koss says. "I explained to her that I did not believe I could do this."

The psychologist reacted in a way that surprised Koss. "Yes, well, we *should* quit," he recalls she said. "We should go and tell your coach that you are not skating because you cannot do this. We agree on this—it's too tough."

Her reaction provoked an immediate retort from Koss: "Of *course* I'm not quitting!" he insisted. "I've never quit anything in my life!"

The two of them, the speed skater and the sport psychologist, devised a path forward. In order to reduce the pressure he felt, Koss had to figure out how to accept the possibility of failure at the Olympics. "That was my number one goal for the five days before the Games," Koss says.

The psychologist helped Koss see that, while the Olympic Games were of course tremendously important, they did not define the rest of his life. Koss had already decided that he wanted to transition into a career as a doctor once his skating career was over. The psychologist asked him, "If you fail at the Olympics, will that make you a bad doctor?" The two of them discussed how failure could actually increase his empathy for people going through tough times—failure at the Olympics might actually make him an even better physician.

That perspective helped alleviate the sense that Olympic failure would cascade through the rest of his life, but it didn't help with the pressure of an entire country counting on his performance. For that, Koss and the psychologist discussed the strength of the Norwegian team. Koss realized that even if he didn't *personally* win, he was on a very good team. The country of Norway didn't particularly care whether it was Koss or another Norwegian who won, so long as the winner was from Norway. That epiphany diffused a little more of the pressure Koss felt—just enough to make it manageable.

As it turned out, a Norwegian did win. His name was Johann Olav Koss. Once he endured his crucible of pressure, Koss delivered one of the most dominant performances in the history of the Olympic Winter Games. In the 5,000-meter event he turned in a world-record time of 6:34.96 to take the gold by more than eight seconds—an eternity in an event where the women's gold medal was decided by half a second. In the 1,500 meters, two days later, Koss won gold in another world-record time. And finally, in the 10,000-meter event, Koss bettered his own world record from three years before by 13 seconds to complete the sweep. Three races, three gold medals, and three world records.

Koss credits his conversation with the sport psychologist as a factor in his success. "It was fascinating—the release of energy it gave me in the four days of preparation for my first race," Koss remembers. "I went from a literally depressed, crying individual under the staircase to a . . . person who tried everything I could in the last four days and then broke the world record on the fifth day."

THE PARADOX OF
IMPORTANCE

Importance plays a unique role in the pressure equation. Essentially, it's a double agent. As we saw in the last chapter, Rick Hansen's deep connection with the importance of his vision of a world without barriers was vital to his ability to persevere through the immense pressure of the Man in Motion World Tour. When it comes to the long haul, importance is like a big log of old oak in the firepit, in that it gives us slow-burning, long-lasting energy. Importance provides conviction in the face of life's inevitable pressures and setbacks.

In peak pressure moments, however, importance can be suffocating. In Koss's experience, the importance of the Olympics was a necessary source of energy during the long, grueling days of training leading up to the Games. But the outsized importance he placed on the outcome eventually became stifling. He let the stakes grow in size until they became not just about the Olympics, but a referendum on who he was as a person and the success of his overall life—past, present, and future.

Over the long haul, we want to ensure that we can connect what we do on a day-to-day basis to why it matters. But in the heat of battle, our task is almost the exact opposite: we must consciously ensure that we aren't ascribing *too much* importance to the event. We need to maintain perspective and seek opportunities to shed the baggage of unnecessary importance. So how do we do that?

STEP 1: ASK YOURSELF ONE KEY QUESTION

We learned in Chapter 2 that our attention narrows under the influence of pressure. In tense situations, we absorb less information than when we are relaxed. So what does the brain tend to focus on in these high-pressure moments? As you would expect, it quite naturally orients to what is at stake. As a sales rep heads into a big sales presentation, she inevitably thinks about the deal that is on the table to win or lose. As an aspiring certified public accountant sits down to write an accreditation exam, he imagines the implications failure might mean for his career. And 20 years ago, as I stared blankly at an incomprehensible twelfth-grade chemistry exam, my mind flashed forward to the tense conversation that awaited when my parents learned of my poor performance.

As we saw with Johann Koss, what's at stake can expand from a speed skating race to the totality of life itself. And so the first tool at your disposal when it comes to managing importance under pressure is to *refocus*—to wrest your brain away from the stakes by asking one deceptively simple question:

WHAT'S *NOT* AT STAKE?

In other words, what are the things in your life that *will not change* regardless of outcome? Ideally, you'll be able to come up with numerous items, anything from the love of your spouse, children, and other family members to the enjoyment of an upcoming cottage weekend, from the pleasure you take in a sunset to the anticipation of an upcoming dinner date at a great restaurant.

Once you have identified the things that *aren't* at stake, the goal becomes to focus on them, holding them front and center in your mind as you approach the event that provoked the pressure in the first place—what I call the moment of impact.

Let's take the earlier example of a sales rep heading into a big presentation. As the presentation approaches, the sales rep becomes acutely aware of the stakes. In fact, the stakes are all she can think about: the revenue opportunity for the business, the impact the sale would have on her compensation, and the potential reputational boost (or hit) if she wins (or loses) the account—which could, in turn, affect her chances for promotion.

To this list of very real stakes, it's possible that she has added some baggage. Perhaps she has come to believe that a loss will somehow signal to her colleagues that she has been faking it all along, that her success to this point has been a mirage—so she's risking the respect of her peers. And maybe she herself has also come to see this presentation as a test. Is she smart enough? Is she good enough? Is this as high as she'll ever advance? Or does she have the ability to progress in her career? At this point, she sees her very self-worth as at stake.

When we're in this frame of mind, we are seeing only a small fraction of the overall picture. It's as if we've zoomed in on one side of a scale without seeing what is balanced on the other side. The easiest way to begin rounding out the picture is to start with the low-hanging fruit: to consciously list the things that are very obviously not at stake. For the sales rep, this list could look like something like the one that follows. No matter how well I perform in this presentation, she might say:

- My children will still love me.
- My parents will still love me.
- My partner will still love me.
- My relationships with my friends will not change.
- My health will stay the same.
- The majority of my compensation won't be impacted—we will be financially secure.
- I'll still have my job.
- We'll still go on the trip we've planned during spring break.

Rosie MacLennan, the two-time Olympic gold medalist, makes writing this list a discipline: "I write down my anchors: my family, my nieces, my husband. They all care if I do well, but only because I care. If I fall on my face, they're going to care if I'm okay. But they don't really care about the outcome. The people who really matter in your life are going to be there regardless."

These other factors provide a counterweight. And sometimes, simply going through this first step is enough to mitigate the pressure one feels.

STEP 2: AVOID THE ANXIETY SPIRAL

At times, however, we need to dig a little deeper. *Yes, it's wonderful that my family will still care about me,* the sales rep might think, *but there remains the prospect of coming into an office full of colleagues who perceive me as a failure and a fraud every single day.* The pressure associated with that prospect still feels unbearable. So the *second* step is to begin to question what we are telling ourselves, asking ourselves, for each item on our list, "Is this *really* at stake?"

Let's consider what you can do the next time you experience an anxiety spiral—that cascading series of emotional dominoes that can see anyone segue from calm performer to panicked paralysis. It can happen to the best of us, even Johann Koss, one of the most dominant athletes ever to compete at the Winter Games. The key difference for you? You likely won't have a sport psychologist around who can talk you down from an anxiety spiral. You have to be your *own* psychologist. So when you feel the anxiety coming on, you want to do three things:

- **Push for data:** Ask yourself, "What evidence do I have to support that this is at stake? Am I *sure* this is in play?"
- **Pretend you're advising someone else, so you can be objective:** For example, ask yourself, "Would I view a person on my team who experienced a similar setback as a fraud?"
- **Give yourself the benefit of the doubt:** If you can't be sure whether something is at stake, ask yourself, "What value is there in assuming this is at stake when I'm not sure?"

As she goes through this exercise, our sales rep might realize that she is unlikely to be seen as a fake or a fraud by the rest of the office. But her self-examination may reaffirm that the outcome of the deal will likely affect her ability to get promoted early. So for her, the scales appear as follows:

AT STAKE	NOT AT STAKE
• Sales commission on the sale/extra compensation • Revenue for the business • Early promotion	• Love and support of family and friends • Support of colleagues • Health • Financial security

Once you've made your list of potential stakes and questioned each one, your view should be more balanced. You are in no way denying that some important things are at stake; the key is simply that you will be able to see the stakes in their appropriate perspective. And when comparing your lists of things at stake versus things not at stake, you will often find that significantly more is stable than is in play.

Perhaps most usefully, there are benefits to focusing on each of the columns at different points in the lead-up to an event. In the sales rep's case, in the weeks prior to her sales meeting, she will likely find it helpful to focus on the fact that winning the deal could lead to an early promotion. That is likely to help give her the energy to put in the hours required to push through all of the prep work and make her presentation as great as it should be. As she moves into performance mode, however, she'll derive more benefit from shifting to the second column and focusing on what's *not* at stake. So how do you know when it's time to switch your focus? Let your body tell you. There is no performance benefit to be gained from an erratic heart rate, fast breathing, and sweaty palms. When those cues arise, it's time to shift focus.

If those biological cues don't manifest but you still feel the butterflies out there, flapping their wings and threatening to transform into a full-blown panic attack, I suggest consciously changing your focus in the moments before your performance. When it's *imminent*. In the seconds prior to kicking off the presentation, taking center stage, or opening your exam booklet. *That's* the time to consciously consider an image of the smiling faces of your kids, or even the cold drink at the bar that awaits you regardless of how things turn out. To recognize that this will soon be over, and some things will have changed, and others will not. Hold the important thing that *will not change* front and center in your mind, and then step into the moment and let it rip.

STEP 3: LET GO OF EGO-DRIVEN STAKES

In 2008, Andrew Blau was tapped to run the iconic consulting firm Global Business Network (GBN). GBN was formed in 1987 by a group of hyper-smart strategists including Peter Schwartz of Royal Dutch Shell and *Whole Earth Catalog* author Stewart Brand. The firm was among the first to use a tool called scenario planning to help organizations prepare for the future. At the time, most consulting firms employed forecasting to extrapolate future possibilities from past trends. Scenario planning involved dreaming up sometimes outlandish "what if" scenarios that could then be used to challenge company orthodoxy and guide strategy. Among GBN's stable of thinkers were *Wired* editor Kevin Kelly and the musician Brian Eno. The approach influenced an entire generation of consultants.

When Blau was asked to step into the CEO role, he felt humbled. It was a big deal to him, he says, "to be asked to lead this organization . . . I wanted to do well. I was stepping into some big shoes, getting a chance to do something that I certainly was honored to be asked to do, and I wanted to do a good job."

The honeymoon was short-lived: Lehman Brothers collapsed 10 days after the leadership transition was announced, and the ensuing financial crisis led to a period of intense pressure that Blau navigated for the next two years. The crisis was particularly bad for GBN, given their focus on helping clients think long term. "I would talk to clients," Blau recalls, "and they'd say, 'If you can change our top line revenue in 90 days, we can talk. It you have anything else to talk about, I don't have time for that right now.'"

As the months passed and the economic climate worsened, the relentless pressure started to affect him. Blau had to make some painful choices. He downsized the company, laying off people who had been his colleagues for years. He felt responsibility for the firm and tried to shoulder the burden himself to protect his coworkers—a sacrifice that ultimately backfired. "I made a choice about a kind of more traditional heroic model of leadership that said I would buffer the stress within myself, [but] in the name of buffering people from stress, I actually *created* stress for them and for me."

Beyond the pressure at work, constant global travel led to pressure at home. He and his wife had two young children. His wife confronted him one day and said she felt like a single mom. "It makes you question, What am I doing?" Blau said. "What does success mean if being the CEO of this company doesn't feel like I'm succeeding?"

Blau realized he was stuck in a classic pressure trap. He had mentally expanded the stakes beyond what was actually in play. He wasn't just navigating an unprecedented crisis, he had also started to think of the situation as a test of his own worth as a leader. Reflecting on that period more than a decade later, Blau notes: "In the work that I do . . . work is a very important part of people's identity, their sense of meaning about the way they contribute or make a difference in the world. So when that is threatened, it's not just the work that feels threatened, it's something deeper."

Blau ultimately dealt with the accumulating pressure of his position by trying to keep his job in perspective. "Maybe the psychic validation I was getting as the head of this storied company was a fake," he thought. "Maybe by the end . . . I wouldn't be the head of the company. Okay. I didn't want that to happen, but if that's the worst thing that happens to you in your life, that's not that big a deal."

As we work through the discipline of determining what is and what isn't at stake, some of the toughest things to categorize are the stakes involving our ego—what Blau calls "psychic validation." Much of the outsized importance that we attach to situations is rooted in how we desire to be seen by others. These stakes are often the ones that cause us the most pressure. In the remarkable book *Awareness*, the irreverent Indian Jesuit priest Anthony de Mello lays bare the challenges of chasing this validation: "Do you like being in prison? Do you like being controlled? Let me tell you something: If you ever let yourself feel good when people tell you that you're okay you are preparing yourself to feel bad when they tell you you're not good. As long as you live to fulfill other people's expectations, you better watch what you wear, how you comb your hair, whether your shoes are polished—in short, whether you live up to every damned expectation of theirs. Do you call that human?"

It can be useful to add this component of ego to the process of determining what's at stake. We often place pressure on ourselves because the result of our endeavor might improve, harm, or otherwise affect others' perception of us. For example, if Johann Koss had failed to win *any* medals in Lillehammer, it's likely true that he would be remembered very differently than he is today. If the sales rep were to blow that presentation, it's possible that might change the way her boss thinks of her. In such cases, we should ask ourselves, "Is this important to *me* or to my ego?" If the answer is your ego, the best course of action is to work to liberate yourself from that pressure, robbing those particular stakes of their power as much as possible. In summarizing the works of psychologist Alfred Adler, the Japanese authors Ichiro Kishimi and Fumitake Koga distill this imperative down to one simple sentence: "Freedom is the courage to be disliked."

STEP 4: GAUGE WHAT IS TRULY URGENT

Once you've done all you can to let go of ego-driven stakes, the final target is manufactured urgency. If ego is the call from inside the house, manufactured urgency is the guy trying to break down the front door.

Booking.com is one of the world's most popular travel sites. In 2016, it was estimated by HOTREC, the trade group of European hospitality businesses, that Expedia and booking.com together capture roughly 80% of overall accommodation bookings in

Europe. When you search booking.com, no matter where or when you are looking to travel, you will be presented with two initial options and then a third option with a big red banner that says "You just missed it! Our last room sold out a few days ago." This pattern—noticed by UX Designer Lauri Lukka and shared in a Medium blog post fittingly titled "Only One Room Left!"—is just one of a vast array of tactics designed by booking.com to create a heightened sense of urgency that forces you to act.

While this is a blatant example, manufactured urgency surrounds us in numerous less-obvious forms. There is manufactured urgency in emails from work colleagues flagged high priority. Breaking news alerts on our phones link to the latest polling data two years out from an election. A text message from a friend prompts an immediate response, even though it diverts our attention from something that's comparatively much more important to complete.

Perhaps the best-known tool for dealing with urgency is the Eisenhower Box (also known as the Eisenhower Matrix), pictured in Figure 4. This tool originated from a quote attributed to American president and former Second World War five-star general Dwight D. Eisenhower: "I have two kinds of problems," he said. "The urgent and the important. The urgent are not important, and the important are never urgent." In using the Eisenhower Box, we are forced to confront whether the issues we are facing are *urgent, important, both,* or *neither.* Often, thanks to the ability of technology and marketing to create a sense of manufactured urgency, we'll discover that we are focusing on the urgent at the expense of the important. We can use the Eisenhower Box as a useful framework for refocusing action and delegating or dropping tasks where appropriate.

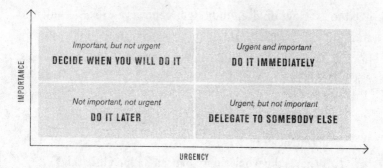

FIGURE 4: *Eisenhower Box*

An honest accounting of whether something is truly important is a great starting point. But how do you decide whether something is truly urgent? In a world where every headline, subject line, and banner ad screams TIME SENSITIVE, it's easy to get swept up in the whirlwind.

Neither Apple nor Google, the two giants who together control 98% of the smartphone operating systems market today, was first to market. In fact, neither was even *second*. They rightly saw that the consequences of forcing action early were greater than delaying and getting it right. Getting their smartphone OS to market was *important*, but it wasn't *urgent*. Apple and Google were able to disregard the urgency that had been manufactured by their competitors, and by the media, to appropriately focus on the task at hand.

Most of us aren't running multinational telecommunications companies, but we often feel the same drive to be "first movers." So how do you recalibrate your internal sense of priority to accurately gauge whether a situation truly is urgent?

A good place to start is to connect with what is at the root of urgency: time pressure. Urgency is based on the belief that you need to act now, or else. Auditing urgency is a process similar to auditing stakes. One great way to do it is to question the assumptions that regulate the relationship between *time* and *consequences*. Ask yourself two questions:

1. What is the worst thing that can happen if I force action *now*?
2. What is the worst thing that can happen if I *delay*?

Sometimes, a yawning chasm will exist between the two sets of consequences. Let's say a father is folding laundry in the family room when he smells smoke from the kitchen. Chances are he will react immediately. He will set down the towel he was folding, rush immediately to the kitchen, and, seeing that there actually is a fire, grab the fire extinguisher and put it out. Had he done an audit of the situational urgency, he would have concluded that his instinct for action was correct. The worst thing that could happen if he acted immediately would be a delay in completing his task of folding the laundry. The worst thing that could happen if he delayed would be having his house burn down. The problem actually was urgent.

In many cases, however, acting immediately may result in consequences that are just as bad, or even worse, than delaying acting. For example, imagine you are cc'd on a customer's email to one of your team members that is flagged as "urgent." The customer has an issue with their service, and they aren't happy about it. Your overriding instinct is likely to reply immediately—to assure them that this isn't acceptable and that you will personally get to the bottom of it. You want to demonstrate responsiveness in order to show them just how much you value the relationship. A quick audit of the stakes, however, may reveal that it's worth waiting until you can review it with your team member. After all, the worst thing that can happen if you delay an hour is that an already irritated client is slightly more miffed. But if you reply immediately without understanding your team member's side of the story, you may later learn that there is a very reasonable explanation for the issue—and by responding without having the complete story, you've created a trust issue with your team member and unrealistic expectations from a troublesome customer that will suck up way more than 60 minutes of your time down the road. In short, the matter isn't actually urgent—it just *feels* that way.

IT'S ALL RELATIVE

Hayley Wickenheiser, a four-time Olympic-gold-medal-winning Canadian hockey player, is held in the same regard as Wayne Gretzky. A larger-than-life photo of Wickenheiser holding the Canadian flag greets visitors from other countries as they enter the customs area at Toronto's Pearson International Airport— Wickenheiser's is the first face they see before they formally cross the border and arrive in the country. After a remarkable 23 years wearing a maple leaf on her chest, she retired in 2017 to plaudits that proclaimed her the greatest woman ever to play the game. In June 2019, she was announced as the headliner for the 2019 Hockey Hall of Fame class, only the seventh woman to enter the hall as a player.

When I asked Wickenheiser to describe her moment of greatest pressure, she talked about the lead-up to the Vancouver

Olympic Games in 2010. At that point she'd already won two gold medals, but this one was on home soil, and the crowds expected nothing less than a third gold. Plus, she was team captain. As she recalls: "The amount of attention that is placed on you in a home Games, as a home athlete, is double or triple what it was when we were competing in 2002 in Salt Lake City or 2006 in Torino." This increased attention made the pressure of the lead-up excruciating: "Stress. Just stress," she remembers, describing her state as "anxious, irritable, restless. I found it to be exhausting and debilitating."

Fast-forward eight years, to 2018, when I spoke with her and she arrived at an unexpected epiphany when she recalled the pressure she had put on herself before Vancouver. By that point she was studying medicine at the University of Calgary, and regularly found herself helping out in the city's emergency rooms, working against time to save human lives. The pressure she placed on herself in these life-and-death situations was completely different from what she had felt as an Olympic athlete. "Why was I so wound up about a gold medal final?" Wickenheiser now wonders. "That was *nothing*."

With the passage of time, Wickenheiser has gained perspective on the pressure she placed on herself years before. "It's all relative," she observes.

That simple summary forms the key technique that helps peak performers navigate peak pressure moments. No one is denying that capturing an Olympic gold medal is important—it's the pinnacle of your life's work, an accomplishment that represents years of blood, sweat, and tears. But at the end of the day, it's just hockey.

Wickenheiser working in the ER is the only scenario in this chapter that features life-and-death stakes. Aside from that, no one was ever in mortal danger. Wickenheiser, Koss, Blau, and our fictional sales rep faced a range of scenarios from common to extreme, but in every case the stakes were confined to—at worst—financial or reputational harm. For most of us, that will be true in most of the high-pressure situations we face. But what happens when the stakes are raised? What if the stakes actually *are* life and death?

The reality is that in most circumstances, even those with extreme stakes, there is *some* benefit to accurately gauging importance. If I am in a situation where I'm worried that I might die, it can, in fact, be helpful to focus on the fact that my family's financial security isn't in jeopardy because we have solid life insurance coverage.

That said, in life-and-death situations, particularly those where your loved ones are in danger, focusing on what's at stake can be highly counterproductive. It is typically better in these cases to focus on a set of tools and techniques that involve handling uncertainty. The discipline of taking direct action around what we can control is what I'll discuss in the following chapter.

CHAPTER 6

—

TAKE DIRECT ACTION

UNCERTAINTY IN PEAK PRESSURE MOMENTS

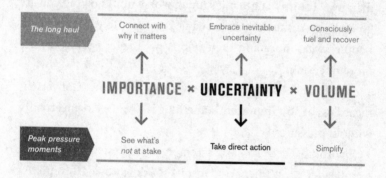

Would you rather experience an electric shock or have a 50% chance of experiencing an electric shock?

On paper, this is a simple choice: take the option where there's a chance of avoiding the shock. Your body, however, sees it differently. In an experiment conducted at University College London, researchers asked participants to turn over virtual rocks on a screen. If there was a snake underneath the rock, the researchers administered an electric shock to the back of the participant's hand. As participants played the game, they came to realize that certain types of rocks always had snakes underneath, others never did, and the remainder were uncertain—sometimes there was a snake, sometimes there wasn't.

For the duration of the experiment, participants were hooked up to biofeedback equipment measuring three markers of activation: the level of cortisol in their saliva, pupil dilation, and sweat. What researchers discovered was unexpected: participants were *less* stressed when they knew they would definitely be shocked, and *more* stressed when there was only a *chance* they would be. In short, as lead author Archy de Berker summarizes: "It turns out that it's much worse not knowing you are going to get a shock than knowing you definitely will or won't. People sweat more and their pupils get bigger when they are more uncertain."

When uncertainty is present, so is pressure. Conversely, regardless of how important something is, there is no uncertainty without pressure.

Dr. Andrew Petrosoniak is an emergency physician and trauma team leader at St. Michael's Hospital in downtown Toronto. As one of only two specialized trauma centers in a metropolitan area of 6.5 million people, St. Mike's sees more than 1,000 trauma cases a year. The majority arrive as transfers from other hospitals' emergency departments when they are deemed too severe to handle. Petrosoniak typically receives anywhere from 10 to 20 minutes' notice to convene his team, decide on a plan, and be ready to receive the patient coming through the door or landing on the helipad.

When I asked about his highest-pressure case, he told me: "The patient had died en route. They had been stabbed in the heart." When there's a wound to the heart, blood collects in the balloon-like sac surrounding it. As the bleeding continues, the pressure stops the heart from beating. "We needed to do a thoracotomy, which is where we open up the chest so you get access to the heart, and then you can relieve the blood that has collected around [it]." A thoracotomy is a very invasive procedure that requires intense coordination among the whole team, but, done correctly, it's immediately lifesaving. "It's the biggest save that you can possibly have, at least in trauma care. It's successful probably around 5% of the time—and it's got to do with when they lost their pulse."

In the case of Petrosoniak's stabbing victim, the pulse had been gone for only a few minutes. There was still a chance to save their life. The trauma surgeon wasn't there yet, but Petrosoniak made the decision to go for it. Anesthesiologists moved to ventilate the patient so that the lungs wouldn't move and obstruct the heart, nurses ran to get blood products and medicate the patient, and another physician inserted a chest tube to ensure there was no additional bleeding from the other side of the chest. Amidst the swirl of activity, Petrosoniak's team made a lifesaving intervention to relieve the pressure and restart the victim's heart, and the trauma surgeon arrived just in time to finish the repair and move the victim to the operating room. Phew.

In reflecting on a career that has had no shortage of pressure, what made this case stand out for Petrosoniak? The situation was critical, but the patient had a chance—even if it was only 5%. "This patient just lost their pulse. They're young. I think we can get them back," Petrosoniak says he was thinking. "It was full-on pressure to act."

He contrasts this case to other more serious ones he's faced where the patient's condition was so dire that, right from the first point of entry, it was clear there was little hope. When it comes to these cases, Petrosoniak notes: "There's not so much pressure there because you're doing anything you can to get them back, but you expect that you won't. When the patient is alive and near death, and you think that there's a potential that you can intervene, *then* there's pressure." In these latter instances, it isn't that the importance has changed—it's still a life on the table—it's the uncertainty that creates pressure.

Many of us find a certain amount of uncertainty enjoyable. It creates a hum of excitement. If you already know how the movie ends, where's the fun in that? Once the uncertainty reaches a certain threshold, however, it moves from being pleasurable and into the realm of physical pain. And in extreme situations, uncertainty can be debilitating.

There are two core imperatives in managing uncertainty in a peak pressure moment:

1. Redirect your attention from what you *can't* control to what you *can* control.
2. Take direct action over what you can control as quickly as possible. The second we start to exert control, the pressure from uncertainty starts to abate.

So far, so good—but control is a funny thing.

THE CONTINUUM OF CONTROL AND THE UNCERTAINTY ZONE

One of the more surprising developments over the past few years has been the rise in popularity of stoicism—a 2,500-year-old philosophy that originated in Athens. Stoicism aims to provide a set of tools for how to live a meaningful and enjoyable life, and was famously embraced by the Roman emperor Marcus Aurelius. Beginning with William B. Irvine's wonderful book *A Guide to the Good Life*, a flood of modern Stoics have published books that aim to apply ancient rules to the modern world.

At the heart of stoicism is a concept that is central to managing uncertainty: the dichotomy of control, which states that the most fundamental task we have as human beings is to separate the things we can control from the things we can't. We must have the discipline to focus our attention and effort entirely on that which we can control or influence. For the original Stoics, this meant focusing relentlessly on our own desires, thoughts, and decisions, and less on worrying about the events unfolding out in the world.

Even if you have no familiarity with the Stoics, this advice may sound familiar. The notion of separating controllables from uncontrollables is baked into schools of thought both sacred and secular, from mindfulness meditation to Zen Buddhism, from Stephen Covey's 7 *Habits of Highly Effective People* to Adlerian psychology. It is a concept that has independently arisen in many different schools of thought and survived thousands of years of scrutiny.

Now, the concept itself seems pretty straightforward. But as always, the devil is in the details. There is a wide gray area between the things we can always control outright and the things over which we never have control. Consider a manager who disagrees with a decision made by executives at her company and is trying to determine whether to agitate or adapt. Clearly, she doesn't have complete control over the situation, but she may think: *There have to be others who see that this is a terrible decision—maybe if we work together we can convince the execs to change their minds.* She may be right, but she may also be wrong. The decision could be a done deal, or it could be open to influence. So how should she decide to act?

Compounding this uncertainty are the Steve Jobses and Elon Musks of the world, and an army of thought leaders fashioned in their image. As Jobs once famously said: "It's the ones who are crazy enough to think they can change the world who actually do." To his way of thinking, it is the people who refuse to accept that things are beyond their control who ultimately have the most profound impact on society. Framed in this light, letting go of the things we can't control (or even acknowledging that there *are* things we can't control) can feel like a form of failure—an abdication of our personal power on the altar of a comfortable life.

This appears to represent a fundamental disconnect between the Stoics, who advocated changing yourself to adapt to the world, and modern-day icons, for whom the greatest good is making a "dent in the universe." So how do we reconcile these two points of view? Let's start with two universal truths.

First, the only things that are *always* within our control are our own thoughts and actions: how we choose to look at a situation and what we choose to do about it. This does not mean that we are always in control of our thoughts and actions, just that we can be. All of us have moments when we get hijacked and our thoughts run away from us or we lash out and act without thinking. But even then, it is always within our control to correct course if we choose to. No one else gets to decide how I feel about a situation or how I respond—I decide. As we'll see as we dive in to the tools in this chapter, connecting with this most fundamental human ability is at the heart of the most productive responses to pressure from uncertainty.

Second, there is one thing that is *never* within our control: other people's thoughts and actions. Ultimately, regardless of what we do, other people get to decide what they think and how they act. The illusion that we can control other people, and the effort we make to exert control, is behind much of what causes us distress. Anthony de Mello memorably sums up our misguided approach to others as "You'd better behave as I have decided or I shall punish myself by having negative feelings." Our attempts to exert control over others often backfire and create additional pressure and pain for us. Other people are not the only thing we can't control, of course—there are natural disasters, technological failures, and butterflies flapping their wings in Tokyo.

Between these extremes of control lies the "uncertainty zone"—the gray area where your ability to reach a particular outcome is in part determined by your own actions and in part out of your control (see Figure 5).

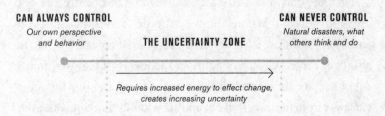

FIGURE 5: *The uncertainty zone*

Take the manager in our previous scenario. It may well be possible for her to rally enough support in the organization to make a case to the executive team and convince them to reverse the decision, but at the end of the day, it may still be out of her control. The executives get to make up their own minds.

Far to the right in the uncertainty zone lie the challenges tackled by people idolized by Steve Jobs, like Mahatma Gandhi, Martin Luther King Jr., and Nelson Mandela. By creating massive movements that motivated thousands of other people to reorder their thoughts and actions, they were able to exert control over situations that millions of others saw no ability to influence. But in all of their cases, success came at tremendous personal cost. Going this far into the uncertainty zone requires connecting with something you believe in so deeply that you are willing to fight tooth and nail to exert influence even when the outcome appears totally out of your control.

When you're in the uncertainty zone, you need to decide how much energy you are willing to spend, and what price are you are willing to pay, to attempt to exert control. The farther to the right you are in the uncertainty zone—where the behavior of others will determine more than your own behavior—the less certain the outcome, and the more energy it will take for you to exert control.

WHAT'S YOUR SERVE?

In normal circumstances, we spend a fair bit of time in the uncertainty zone. We worry about the work ethic of the rest of our team on projects at work, spending energy to put systems in place to ensure we have regular check-ins on their progress; we check the weather daily in the week leading up to our child's outdoor birthday party, worrying that the icon in the weather app will flip from sunbeam to thunderbolt; we gently ask our partner at home to please, for the love of God, not leave their dishes in the sink for the 100th time.

In peak pressure moments, we need to keep our focus squarely on the things we can control. For one thing, we have limited ability to spend the extra energy necessary to exert control in the gray area when we are already under extreme pressure. But more importantly, focusing on things outside of our control leads to a feeling of helplessness. Nothing compounds the negative impact of pressure like helplessness, the feeling that "nothing I do will make a difference."

The opposite of helplessness is self-efficacy. First described by legendary Stanford psychologist Albert Bandura, self-efficacy is your belief in your own ability to have an impact on your circumstances. Connecting with self-efficacy is what transforms the experience of uncertainty from one of threat to one of challenge and control. When we begin to focus on the things we control, we build our sense of self-efficacy and start to reduce the weight of uncertainty.

In this way, where we direct our focus can either start a reinforcing cycle that magnifies the impact of uncertainty, or it can give us an off-ramp that reduces uncertainty and therefore the impact of pressure (see Figure 6).

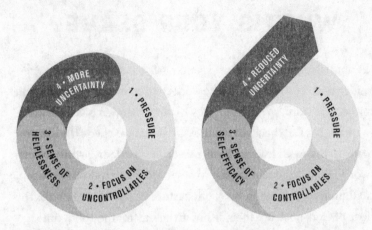

FIGURE 6: *Focus on uncontrollables (left) versus focus on controllables (right)*

One of my favorite stories on this topic comes from a conversation I had with Martin Reader, an Olympic beach volleyball player. Reader and his partner, Josh Binstock, were working to qualify for the 2012 London Games. With just over a month left before the Games, they headed to the NORCECA Continental Cup Finals, held in Mexico in June 2012, with their Olympic dreams on the line. It was simple: win the tournament and they were in. After defeating Cuba in the semifinals, they faced a challenging Mexican team with the strong support of a boisterous hometown crowd in the finals. The Canadian side won the first game 21–17, but the Mexicans came charging back in Game 2 to win 21–11, setting up a winner-take-all third game. Deep into a tight Game 3, with the uncertainty of an Olympic berth in the balance, Reader returned to what he could control: "The only time that you have full control of the situation is when you are holding the ball behind the service line. Everything that happens in the serve is under your control: it has nothing to do with the stadium, the crowd, the officials, or the rally."

For months, Reader had been preparing for this exact situation. In anticipation of meeting the Mexican team in the finals, and recognizing a weakness that they could exploit, he and Binstock had practiced a serve that would allow them to exert total control when they needed it most. "In the final, critical moment, I served an ace that they had no idea was coming. I moved to a totally different spot on the service line and delivered a serve that I had trained for months in advance." And it worked. The Canadians won the third game 15–13 and punched their ticket to London. "That single serve, where I took control of the situation, was the difference between making it to the Olympics or not. And that was six months of preparation for a single service, and that made all the difference."

So, when you are under pressure, consider the following question:

WHAT'S YOUR SERVE?

That is, what is the thing that *right now* is completely within your control. In any situation, there is always a serve. To some extent, your answer will differ depending on the situation—for navy SEAL Curt Cronin, it was calling in the helicopters; for Reader, it was a literal serve. Regardless of the situation, however, there are three things over which you can *always* exert control: your routines, your breathing, and your perspective. These "serves" can be valuable allies when uncertainty comes to call.

USE RITUALS AND ROUTINES TO CREATE PREDICTABILITY

The story of Dr. Petrosoniak's remarkable save didn't start when the patient arrived at the hospital but in the minutes beforehand, when Petrosoniak did what he always does: pre-brief with the team. "To combat the pressure that comes with these situations, we always try to script out the first five minutes," says Petrosoniak. This gives him and the team a sense of both alignment *and* control. They know exactly what their roles are and can focus entirely on executing the routine. In addition to scripting out the first five minutes, they review key decision points. One of these points is almost always the loss of a pulse. "We say, 'Okay, if the patient does not have a pulse or they lose a pulse, we are going to do X.' That's very helpful for the entire team and me to then hold myself accountable to what I might do."

Inherent in this approach to pre-briefing is a recognition that uncertainty cannot fully be tamed. The patient may lose their pulse regardless of the team's best efforts—what's important is that the team is clear on what their accountability is in that moment.

Routines that create stability in the face of uncertainty are part of every elite athlete's toolkit. Tennis players have a routine they follow before serving the ball, basketball players have a routine before taking free throws. Brian Orser, an Olympic medalist in figure skating and now one of the world's most successful coaches, told me about the routines he used as an athlete to mitigate the uncertainty around skating order. In skating competitions, athletes are put into groups of six who all warm up together, but the skating order is drawn randomly just before the skaters take the ice. As a result, following the warm-up you might stay out on the ice and compete immediately, or you could have a 40-minute wait while five other skaters compete and receive their scores.

"We had a skating first routine, a skating second routine, a skating sixth routine," says Orser. And it was detailed. For example, if the athlete was skating sixth: "As you come off the ice, you take off your skates, get settled into the chair, and do some breathing.

Boom—Skater 1 done. Then you have a plan for Skater 2—maybe doing some movement in the hallway. Skater 3, we start doing more energized jumping or fitness moves to get energy up. Skater 4, we walk through the program. At the end of Skater 4, we're going to put our skates on. Now Skater 5 is halfway through their program and we're ready to go on the ice. And the time goes by like that."

Routine gives you a simple way to redirect your attention from outcomes—Will the patient live or die? Will I win or lose this competition?—to behaviors. This shift is at the heart of the continuum of control, but without a routine in place it can be much harder. In the absence of a clear set of steps to follow, our attention naturally gravitates to the outcome or goal we are working toward. So how do you identify a routine that will work for you?

First, you'll want to identify the peak pressure moments in your life that would benefit from the implementation of a routine. For Dr. Petrosoniak, peak pressure is when a trauma patient shows up in the ER; for Orser, it is the period immediately prior to taking the ice. Routine is most beneficial when it is attached to a moment that will occur semi-regularly. In your work this might mean presenting to a crowd, executing a demo of your product, nailing a sales call, or performing a complicated procedure.

Next, reflect on a time when you executed flawlessly (or, if you're a perfectionist, really well). What can you remember about what you did just before that exceptional performance? Did you pace the halls? Sit quietly and run through what you were about to do? Clear your mind? Chew your nails? Whatever you remember about your actions leading up to that exceptional performance can serve as the basis for the first prototype of your routine.

Finally, build in some flexibility. In line with Orser's approach to skating order, you will want to have a routine in place for different scenarios that might occur. If you don't know the order of the presentations to your key client, have a routine for going first, second, or last. Thinking through the different plans in advance will immediately alleviate uncertainty.

Routines can pay big dividends when we have advance knowledge that we are going to face a peak pressure moment and have some time to plan. But how do we exert control when we are thrust into peak pressure moments with no warning? For that, we turn to our next two tools: breathing and perspective.

FOCUS ON YOUR BREATHING

In 1992, Tracy Wilson, an Olympian turned sports commentator, was hired by NBC to do sideline reporting at the Major League Baseball All-Star Game. Her focus would be on human- and special-interest stories that would add color to the broadcast. As the seventh-inning stretch approached, Wilson got an assignment through her earpiece: she was asked to head up to the luxury box level and get ready to conduct a live-to-air interview with then President George H.W. Bush. As Wilson describes it, she panicked. With less than 20 minutes' notice, she had almost no time to prepare questions, and as she followed security up to the box, a steady dose of instructions about timing and topics that were okay and off-limits were being shouted directly into her ear.

As she stood outside the door to the president's box, frantically running through the questions she planned to ask and feeling highly unprepared to perform in front of an audience of millions, Wilson began to notice that the Secret Service agents stationed at the door were looking at her strangely. Pulled out of the frantic monologue in her head, Wilson suddenly realized that she had unconsciously returned to the strategy that had served her so well as an athlete: dressed in high heels and a pantsuit, she was sitting in a deep squat and taking deep belly breaths, one after another. Unperturbed, Wilson focused on her breathing, as she had done for years as an elite athlete. When the door opened, she was able to walk in and nail it.

When everything else is uncertain, focus on your breathing. It's something you can always control. In fact, breathing is one of only two things we do as human beings that is both automatic *and* can be consciously controlled (blinking is the other). Under peak pressure, our breathing can be an ally if we channel it effectively, or it can run away from us and starve our bodies of the oxygen we need to perform (or, in extreme cases, stay conscious). There is a reason that "Take a deep breath" is the first thing we usually say to people who are panicking.

Focusing on breathing serves two purposes: first, it establishes a beachhead of control in the midst of uncertainty that begins to connect us with self-efficacy; second, it has a direct impact on our physiology. Conscious breathing in peak pressure moments can lower our heart rate and move us into a state of coherence. You may remember from Chapter 2 that coherence is a state in which our heart rate synchronizes with our breathing, rising as we breathe in and falling as we breathe out. It is a state that is highly correlated with both high performance and well-being. In fact, when we regularly get into a state of coherence, we increase our heart rate variability, which is a key marker of the heart's ability to adapt and respond to stressors and is strongly correlated with a wide array of health outcomes, including all-cause mortality. Coherence also promotes alpha brain waves, which are correlated with an aware, alert state, while appearing to dampen the high beta waves that are associated with a racing or busy brain.

To access the benefits of coherence, there is one maxim to remember:

BREATHE LOW AND BREATHE SLOW.

In normal situations, most of us tend to breathe somewhere around 12 to 13 breaths per minute. When we become activated, our breathing gets faster and moves from our diaphragm up into our chest. This shift reduces the amount of carbon dioxide (which is a tranquilizer) in our bodies, which in turn reinforces our heightened activation. Breathing low and slow means moving your breathing back down to your diaphragm and slowing it to around 6 breaths per minute. Both of these are counter to what your body automatically does in high-pressure situations, but they remain within your control if you consciously focus on them.

How slow is 6 breaths per minute? Try it for yourself. Grab a stopwatch and time your breathing so that each breath takes 10 seconds, ideally inhaling slightly faster than you exhale. If you're like most people, this will feel painfully slow. At first, it can feel like you aren't getting enough oxygen in your system. With practice, however, this state—and all of its associated benefits—can become second nature, or even unconscious, as in Tracy Wilson's case.

Like any skill, coherent breathing requires practice. I recommend downloading one of the many apps available that give you a breathing pacer (HeartRate+ Coherence is a good, inexpensive option). Practicing breathing at 6 breaths per minute using the pacer will start to give you a good internal sense of what it feels like. Over time, you'll find that you are able to much more easily gauge your breathing level and self-adjust to bring it down appropriately.

RECOGNIZE THAT YOUR PERSPECTIVE IS ALWAYS IN YOUR CONTROL

When Sean St. John was 25 years old, he was on a roll: "I was a couple of years out of university, and I was the first person in my family to go to university." With no contacts in the finance industry whatsoever, St. John had managed to work his way up from the back office of a mutual fund company to a coveted position on the bond trading desk at a prestigious firm. "I was thrilled . . . I thought to myself, *You're here. This is your opportunity. You got to this spot and now you need to get to work.*"

Six months later, St. John was at a music festival with friends when something went devastatingly wrong. After a friend playfully hoisted him on their shoulders, blood started pooling under his skin, starting in his groin and moving up into his stomach. His friends quickly got him into an ambulance. In the ambulance they pumped him full of morphine as they sped through the countryside to the nearest hospital. The reception at the hospital was not comforting. "The doctor came in and looked at me and said, 'Whoa. I've only seen this in books before—I've never seen anything like this,'" St. John remembers. Finally, the doctor came in with a combination of good news and bad news: they could operate and take care of the rupture, but before the surgery, St. John would need to sit and wait for four agonizing hours until the morphine was completely out of his system. "It was excruciating pain," he says.

The surgery was a success, and St. John returned home two days later. Then, about two weeks later, he received a devastating phone call. A biopsy taken during the surgery had revealed a bigger problem: "They said, 'You have testicular cancer. You need to make an appointment at the Princess Margaret Cancer Centre.'" As St. John recalls, "I didn't even know what testicular cancer was, to be honest. I had never even heard of it or known anybody that had gone through it." Even worse, because of some unexplained spots in St. John's lungs and kidneys, doctors feared that the cancer had already spread.

In a moment like this, the uncertainty is untamable and overwhelming. The cancer may respond to treatment, or it may not. It may have already spread to your lungs, but you'll have to wait until your appointment to find out. Your career may need to be put on hold. There is nothing you can do in the moment to reduce the uncertainty; it will only be resolved over time.

And yet, amidst all of this uncertainty, St. John found one thing he could control: his own perspective. "When I was told I needed to have the treatment, I just remember thinking, Okay, well, life's been really good so far. I grew up in a good family, had lots of opportunities, did well in school, and here I am working at one of the best firms, in a career that is hard to get into. So, this is what the test is going to be. This is what you want me to face."

Even as everything else was a blur, St. John was able to maintain control over how he looked at the situation. "I don't remember walking to the hospital, I don't remember the first meeting, I just remember thinking, Okay, let's face it. Get up, get back on the horse." And his ability to exert control over his perspective made a huge difference to how the pressure impacted him relative to how it impacted others. "My parents almost separated over it, and there was a lot of anxiety in the family and a lot of worry with other people, but I don't ever remember having fear myself."

In his landmark book *Man's Search for Meaning*, Viktor Frankl, an Austrian psychiatrist interred in the Nazi concentration camps in the Second World War, wrote about a remarkable discovery he made in the midst of unimaginable suffering. He describes his realization that the Nazis could take away almost everything— clothing, food, shelter—but the one thing they couldn't take away was his ability to choose to see what he was going through as a meaningful experience. He called this "the last human free- dom." For him, meaning came from a determination to survive the camp so that he could tell people what had happened. He writes that he would close his eyes and vividly picture himself at the front of a university classroom after the war, educating people on the horrors of the Holocaust. Outside of himself, he observed that those around him who were able to make this choice—to choose a perspective that framed what they were going through as meaningful—were more resilient through their ordeal.

Changing our perspective is *always* an option if we have the awareness and courage to seize it.

When all we can control is how we look at a situation, it helps to have a few go-to questions that can help us reorient from a perspective of threat and uncertainty to one that is balanced and progress-oriented. Here are three that I've found work well in peak pressure moments:

1. **What am I learning right now?** Even in the most dire situations there is always an answer to this ques- tion. You may be learning creativity, or patience, or

humility, or simply empathy for people who have gone through similar experiences in their lives.

2. **What is the easiest thing I can do right now to make progress?** Reorienting your perspective to focus away from what is happening to you and toward how you can move forward (even if it's a baby step) is always helpful. The answer to this question may be "breathe."

3. **What would XX do?** Imagery is a powerful tool for action in peak pressure moments. Even if we feel entirely out of our depth or lost, we can often picture someone we know who we think would handle the situation well. Once you can picture how they would handle the situation, you have the information you need to begin making progress.

WHEN YOU LACK CONTROL, FOCUS ON WHAT YOU *DO* CONTROL

If you were trying to make up a situation that embodies a lack of control, it would be hard to do better than what Jenn Cruz experienced. Cruz, a human resources leader with a government agency, was responsible for planning a high-stakes meeting for over 150 people, many of whom were dialing in remotely. Just prior to the meeting, the company had announced significant layoffs, some of which she had to communicate personally. The people coming into the meeting weren't sure whether they still had jobs, and they were understandably anxious. As the meeting was set to start, the audio/video failed. No one could join by phone. Her tech team was nowhere to be found; they were at one of the other four identical meetings happening simultaneously elsewhere in the building. Cruz tore down the hall to find them and took a shortcut through a fire escape. When the door closed, she heard an ominous click behind her. Frantically, she grabbed the handle—it was locked.

While this might sound like the kind of story that ends when you wake in a cold sweat, it was not a dream, and was, in fact, only a small part of Cruz's tough day. Cruz had been tapped by senior leaders to orchestrate the communication of a major reorganization following a merger. The merger had been announced six months earlier, and people in the agency had been waiting on pins and needles since then. As part of a highly orchestrated day, there were to be dozens of one-on-one conversations from 9 to 12 in the morning with the individuals being let go, and then five simultaneous regional meetings, all run out of one building, to communicate the changes to the hundreds of remaining employees. After months of planning, it was game day. Cruz herself had had to let four employees go in the morning—something she had never done before. "It was an extremely emotional day, even just to get to 1 p.m," Cruz recalls.

Just before 1 p.m., 300 anxious people filed into four different levels of the meeting facility, with 100 more sitting restlessly by their phones, ready to dial in and learn their fate. One o'clock arrived. The A/V failed. The boss got angry. Cruz ran for the stairwell.

"I remember when I was running toward the stairwell my mind was racing, but I also couldn't think at the same time. It was like my focus narrowed to the point I couldn't even see the possibility of what to do next. All I knew was: I need to get to the A/V people. It was a crazy feeling, having my mind race and not actually have it compute anything—not knowing what to do and not being able to function." In this moment of sheer panic, Cruz flew into the stairwell and the door clicked shut behind her.

After trying the door unsuccessfully, Cruz realized she had no cell reception where she was. Frantically running up and down the stairs, she found another level where she was able to get a single bar, and she called her colleague Brandon, who was in the building. He had one simple piece of advice: "I'll get there. Just take a deep breath." As Cruz recalls, "I remember when he said that because that's when I realized that I wasn't breathing." So, as she sat and waited for him to arrive from another part of the building, that's what she did: "I took a few deep breaths and I thought, *Okay, I can't do anything. So what can I do? Let me breathe, let me think this through.* And actually, that's when Plan B came to me."

By the time Brandon arrived, Cruz had a plan. They sprinted back to the meeting room, where the A/V team was now working frantically. Cruz told the team to try for 10 minutes and if it still wasn't working, they were going to move to one of the rooms that would be vacated by then. After 10 minutes, that's what they did. The attendees joined in the new room and the meeting proceeded—mission accomplished.

It wasn't a good day for Cruz. "I felt really, really horrible for the rest of the day. I went home that evening and I cried for an hour. I couldn't stop crying. It's never really happened to me before. I think it was that accumulation of stress and anxiety that had been building up that I hadn't let myself feel."

And yet it could have been a lot worse. "I don't even know what would have happened if I didn't get locked in that stairwell, to be honest. I probably would have just kept running around that building." Beyond giving her time to clarify her next steps instead of running aimlessly, being stuck in the stairwell allowed her to get her emotions under control: "I think at that point I was just pure, raw emotion. I wasn't thinking properly. All I knew was that this was happening, it needed to get fixed. I am being blamed for this. I'm going to kill this A/V guy. I'm going to kill this guy and his team."

The stairwell forced Cruz to focus on what she could control. She couldn't control the A/V (or the A/V guys!), but she could control her breathing, and her plan for the meeting. Once she had command of those two things, she was able to act. It was a moment of forced clarity.

Even without the benefit of a stairwell to get locked into, we can all learn to get better at figuring out what we can control—and taking action once we have it figured out.

CHAPTER 7

EMBRACE INEVITABLE UNCERTAINTY

UNCERTAINTY OVER THE LONG HAUL

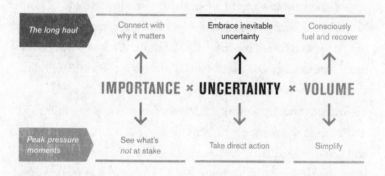

The long haul	Connect with why it matters	Embrace inevitable uncertainty	Consciously fuel and recover
	↑	↑	↑
	IMPORTANCE ×	**UNCERTAINTY** ×	**VOLUME**
	↓	↓	↓
Peak pressure moments	See what's *not* at stake	Take direct action	Simplify

As Olivia Fox Cabane and Judah Pollack outline in their thought-provoking book *The Net and the Butterfly*, the human brain has evolved to respond to uncertainty in a similar way as to pain. We therefore look to minimize uncertainty as much as possible. But here's the truth: we are all en route to death, to misfortunes we haven't considered, to ups and downs that are both unforeseen and unavoidable. No matter how clean we live and how careful we are, uncertainty exists that we can't mitigate. The working world is rife with untamable uncertainty at the hands of the forces of disruption. Controlling uncertainty with direct action is a smart strategy during peak pressure moments, but trying to do so over the long haul can actually backfire because it can create a sense of helplessness, which only increases the pressure.

At 45 years old, Luc Mongeau was on top of the corporate world. In the span of nine years at Mars, Incorporated, he had risen from being an assistant brand manager to become chief marketing officer for their $9 billion Petcare business. It was a career trajectory that was almost unheard of in the consumer-packaged goods industry. Mongeau, a brash, openly gay French Canadian who would show up to work in a Ferrari, dressed head to toe in Louis Vuitton and Burberry, was well suited to the meteoric rise. "All my life I had been fueled by external validation. What was drilled into me at a young age was that financial success is the ultimate validation—it's the ultimate achievement that gets you respect."

Respect was important to Mongeau. It was something that had been in short supply early in his life. More open than almost any senior executive I've ever spoken with, Mongeau is incredibly transparent about his journey: "I grew up never feeling good enough—never thinking that my father recognized my value. I was a younger brother to a guy who was an overachiever in sports— Olympic volleyball team, tryouts for [MLB's Montreal] Expos. And I had no coordination, was fairly heavy as a kid, and from the time I was eight years old, I knew I was gay." Determined to prove his worth to his father and the world, Mongeau became incredibly driven: "I was fueled by that 'fuck you energy.' It was always like 'Fuck you, I'm going to show you that I'm good enough. Fuck you, I'm going to show you I'm better than you.'"

The plan appeared to be working—until it didn't. Six months after his promotion into the global CMO role, Mongeau's time at Mars came to an abrupt end. It was an acrimonious exit with a protracted fight over severance. When the battle was over, Mongeau went back home, assuming that he would take some time off and then reemerge to pick up where he'd left off. But there was a problem: the "fuck you energy" that had fueled his rise had also led to burnt bridges on the way out, and it proved harder than expected for him to come back. One year off turned into two and then three and eventually four. As interview after interview failed to pan out, Mongeau's inner monologue began to take on a different tone. "I'd been off for years as a result of what I considered to be a failure. So the tape in the back of my head started to say, 'It was a fluke that got you there, and you got found out.' And that tape was reinforced when I would go to interviews and it was rejection after rejection after rejection."

Four years after his exit, Mongeau made a bold decision: he would fly to Amsterdam and try to get a meeting with the person who had fired him. "I had screwed up with it," he says. "I had been fairly nasty to him when I got fired, and he was in my head as a strong contributor to the negative tape that was playing." Against the odds, he got a meeting. And it was transformative. "I sat down with him and said, 'I see my responsibility here and I sincerely want to apologize for that. And here's what I've done to get better.' I had to eat a lot of humble pie." In the face of this vulnerability, not only did his ex-boss agree to put it behind them, he also started to talk about the qualities he had seen in Mongeau that had led him to get promoted so quickly in the first place: his leadership acumen, his energy, his instincts. Flying home from Amsterdam, Mongeau now had two tapes playing in his head.

With a renewed sense of optimism, and—equally important—the resuscitation of a key reference, Mongeau went back on the job hunt. Shortly after that, five full years after his ignominious exit from Mars, he was offered the chief executive officer role at Weston Foods, a multibillion-dollar bakery based in Toronto and a key holding of one of Canada's most prominent families, the Westons. He was back in the game. Mongeau saw it as more than just a job, however. "For me, coming back to work, I took on the added pressure of showing the world that I wasn't a loser. I was thinking, Mongeau is a winner, he's not a loser, and he's going to show you that with what he's going to do with this business."

Priding himself on his ability to push a business forward quickly, Mongeau and his team started to draft a major reorganization of the business around a new strategy. "I came up with the idea of collapsing all of the business units together; it was a major re-org that flipped the organization upside down." Ten months after he assumed the CEO role, and with the owners supportive but cautious, they flipped the switch in November 2017. It was a path that would rewrite a majority of the job descriptions in the business, upend reporting relationships, and—if all went according to plan—lead the business forward on modern underpinnings after a period of initial managed chaos. But the timing could not have been worse.

On January 31, 2018, a bomb dropped: "Documents reveal Canada Bread, Weston as key players in bread-price-fixing scheme," read the headline in Canada's largest newspaper, the *Globe and Mail*. In what would become one of the biggest news stories of the year, it was revealed that for 14 years prior to Mongeau's arrival, employees at Weston had been working with other bakeries, and all of the large grocery chains, to fix the price of bread for consumers, locking in price inflation that was double the rate of increases seen by American consumers. Given the dominant position of the players involved, this meant that almost every single person in Canada had been a victim of the arrangement. Weston's sister company Loblaws, Canada's largest grocer, went into damage control mode, offering all 35 million Canadians a $25 gift card by simply registering online. A $1 billion class-action lawsuit was launched on behalf of Canadians, and the story stayed in the news for over a year.

Later, documents revealed something both morally encouraging and practically challenging for Mongeau: the original whistleblower in the scandal was actually Weston's owner, Galen Weston Jr. On discovering evidence of price-fixing within his own organization, Galen flagged the issues with the competition bureau. Morally, it was the right thing to do, but it also made things tricky at Weston, which had as customers both the very grocery chains that had been highlighted as part of the scandal and many other key retail customers that Weston had been doing business with for years. Add in historical supply issues at Weston and self-inflicted wounds due to the strategic transformation, and some difficult conversations arose. "I remember going into a meeting with one of our biggest customers," recalls Mongeau. "We were called there in person so they could say, 'Hey, guys—we're delisting all of your products.' We were sitting in a tiny, cramped conference room and realizing that was $40 million in business right there. And I mean, there were multiple meetings like that."

As the business outlook got worse and worse, the pressure started to cascade. "It was a perfect storm," says Mongeau. "We've collapsed the entire organization, everybody is in a new role, nobody knows if they're coming or going, and then you go through period after period after period where we have to call down the numbers." With the hits coming fast and furious, Mongeau's inner narrative reverted to an unhelpful place. "Every night I would go home and I would think, *I am really not up to this job. My judgment isn't good. My strategic acumen isn't good.*" This doubt manifested as a relentless drive to turn things around even in the face of circumstances outside of his control. "I was extremely tense. I was tense at work, I was tense at home. It was impacting my relationship with my kids and my partner just because I was so bloody tense."

At the peak of the pressure, with the business in a state of disarray, customers canceling orders, and his self-worth in doubt, Mongeau got a tap in the right direction. "I was walking by [my head of HR's] desk in the morning, and she could tell that I was tense. She's always been a good copilot—not afraid of telling me when I'm doing something wrong. And she just said, 'Luc, you're doing a great job. The situation is just the situation. You need to just let go.' And I vividly remember just this little five-minute conversation—I can replay it in my head even today." That tiny, seemingly innocuous intervention reconnected Mongeau with something that had helped sustain him through his five years without a job. "I had a lot of time on my hands. I would wake up at 8 a.m. on Monday and think, *I've got to get through the entire day. These days are so long.* And despair could set in. So I studied Buddhism quite a bit. And I got to a place—it's going to sound very touchy-feely—but I got to a place where I could just have faith that everything will be okay. To just embrace the situation with a faith and belief that everything will be okay." In reflecting on a really tough 2018, he sees it as a parallel situation: "Honestly, I think it's that mindset that got me through the year. Not faking that everything will be perfect, but just embracing it and having faith in my capabilities and faith that, in the end, everything will be okay."

Part of his shift came from seeing beyond the tunnel vision of what was at stake at work to what was *not* at stake—similar to what we saw in Chapter 5: "If I've got the love of all of these people around me, I must be worth something. So, whether this is successful or not, at the end of this there's my husband and my kids. And that's wealth." It also helped that Mongeau's mindset was echoed and supported by his leaders. "My boss was always patient, always supportive. He would say, 'You guys are doing the right things. I wouldn't do anything different. Let's just keep pushing.'"

That shift in mindset also shifted everything else. "That day I went from a tense, negative mindset of 'I'm going to get the fuckers—and everyone out of my way' to embracing the situation. My attitude completely changed." The uncertainty hadn't abated, but reconnecting with the mindset of embracing uncertainty that had helped Mongeau navigate five years between roles also helped him manage the intense pressure of a tough year, and ultimately turn the tide.

THE PARADOX OF UNCERTAINTY

Embedded in Mongeau's story is something that I heard repeatedly in my interviews about pressure over the long haul, and that I started to realize embodied a paradox of uncertainty. Staying energized when you're experiencing uncertainty over the long haul requires simultaneously holding two seemingly incompatible mindsets:

- accepting that the future is uncertain, unknown, and unknowable; *and*
- having faith that everything will work out okay in the end.

Being able to simultaneously understand that the future is uncertain and unknowable (and therefore uncontrollable) *and* have a patient belief that everything will work out the way it should in the end is a powerful and challenging combination. It's not something that most of us can hold to 100% of the time. As we saw with Mongeau, it was a mindset he practiced deeply during a very difficult period in his life but that he had to relearn when he was confronted with a new wave of pressure. It's a lesson that he has to work hard to hold on to on a daily basis. And yet the benefits of practicing this mindset over the long haul are immense.

LEARN TO LOVE SURPRISES

The previous chapter introduced the idea of separating what we can control from what we can't, and the big gray "uncertainty zone" in the middle. The simple reality is that, with so many things out of our control or only partially within our control, we cannot know or dictate the future. Attempting to tame all of the uncertainty in our lives is a recipe for burnout—a long, slow journey toward finally acknowledging the limits of our control. For Mongeau, this acceptance took a tap on the shoulder, a simple reminder that "the situation is what it is." An elite male tennis player born in 1985 has to accept that he's playing in the era of Roger Federer, Rafael Nadal, and Novak Djokovic, and there is nothing he can do to change their innate talent and incredible work ethic.

When we try to take direct action on what we can control over the inevitable uncertainty of the long haul, we layer on a feeling of helplessness. It's almost like we are trying to tighten a nut with a wrench that doesn't fit. Nowhere is this more prevalent than in business, where the tools of action that most people have learned are rooted in a strong bias to optimize for efficiency, predictability, and compliance.

Melissa Quinn, the managing director of transformation at the consultancy firm Edelman and the former chief operating officer of Doblin, Deloitte's global innovation practice, has a terrific way of talking about this. Quinn and I met many years ago when we were both working at The Monitor Group, a consulting firm founded by legendary strategist Michael Porter and five Harvard colleagues. With its heritage of leading thinkers in strategy and business, Monitor tackled client work with what Quinn calls a "classic hypothesis-driven approach." Faced with a challenge—say, a client looking to determine how to enter a new foreign market— Monitor teams would spend a short time diverging to come up with a few different ideas of what the "answer" could be. In this situation, for example, it could be creating a wholly owned subsidiary, buying a local firm, or establishing a joint venture. After this short period of divergence, the team's focus would shift to the main phase of the project: using data to determine which answer was the correct one and making a recommendation.

In 2007 Monitor acquired Doblin, a boutique innovation consulting firm based in Chicago. Founded by designer Jay Doblin, the firm was one of the first to recognize that the process used to design physical objects like chairs or coffee mugs could be applied to solving business problems. The rise of what became termed "design thinking" reshaped corporate innovation. After the transaction was finalized, Quinn was tapped to lead the integration of Doblin into Monitor. She moved to Chicago with her husband, Brian, and got ready to tackle the exciting mandate of marrying the best strategic thinking with the best design thinking.

The issues started to arise almost as soon as the first projects launched with mixed teams of Monitor and Doblin consultants. "I'd have Monitor people coming into my office going, 'What is wrong with these Doblin guys? They just want to sit around and *talk*. We're not making any progress toward the answer at all.' And then I'd have Doblin people coming into my office saying, 'What is wrong with these Monitor guys? All they care about is getting to an answer immediately—and we don't even understand the problem yet!'"

The conflict, Quinn quickly realized, was rooted in the values embedded in two different approaches to solving problems. Whereas the Monitor approach valued quickly dissecting the problem and laying out a predictable path to a solution among an established set of potential answers, the design-led Doblin approach valued exploration—pursuing a much longer period of divergence in which the designers were open to new information, looking for things that might surprise them, and working to more deeply understand the core problem they were trying to solve. Only once they had lived in this uncertain period of exploration for a prolonged period of time would they feel comfortable enough to start converging on a solution. In her daily quasi-therapy sessions with exasperated consultants, Quinn started sketching out a visual that laid out the tension in approaches that was leading to disconnects within her teams:

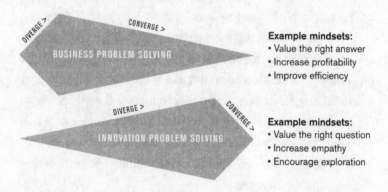

BUSINESS PROBLEM SOLVING
DIVERGE >
CONVERGE >

Example mindsets:
- Value the right answer
- Increase profitability
- Improve efficiency

INNOVATION PROBLEM SOLVING
DIVERGE >
CONVERGE >

Example mindsets:
- Value the right question
- Increase empathy
- Encourage exploration

The traditional business approach to solving problems is exactly what is needed in peak pressure moments—it lets us immediately hone in on what we can control and take action. Over the long haul, however, with all of its unknowns and inevitable uncertainty, there are many situations in which we need to take the alternate path—the one that opens us up to surprises, encourages exploration, and doesn't immediately attempt to drive toward answers and action. Bob Lurie, a valued mentor of mine and a true strategic genius who is currently the vice president of corporate strategy at Eastman Chemical, spent a large portion of his career building a marketing consultancy called Market2Consumer (M2C) into a $100 million revenue business. When I talked to him about it, he told me the team started with a list of over 40 potential products, ranked from most to least promising. It took them until number 27 to get the business off the ground. Their top 26 ideas, painstakingly considered and carefully executed, didn't resonate with the market. But number 27, which was a novel approach to customer segmentation, ended up being a $100 million product. Lurie's advice to me was straightforward: "You don't have the answers, and you can't predict what is going to work."

I've thought about this advice often ever since, and it has been among the most useful reminders for me personally. Each time one of my brilliant ideas turns out to not be so brilliant after all, I imagine Lurie scratching one more product off the list and moving on to the next, having learned something and ultimately recognizing that we can't tame or predict uncertainty, but we can expect it and get through a period of uncertainty without becoming dispirited or disengaged.

For Quinn's part, she started working to help people embrace new mindsets that helped them both see the possibility in and value uncertainty and exploration. "Mindsets are like cross-country ski tracks in the snow," Quinn says. "Over time they get grooved in and we just unconsciously follow along because deviating takes effort." She started codifying a set of what she called business mindsets and innovation mindsets, and asking people to become aware of which they were holding when tackling problems. She then encouraged them to consciously "groove in" the opposing mindset to see how that would change their behavior.

BUSINESS MINDSETS	INNOVATION MINDSETS
Value the right answer	Value the right question
Improve efficiency	Encourage exploration
Use data & logic to inspire confidence	Use prototypes & stories to inspire confidence
Learn, create, assess	Create, assess, learn
Plan and predict results	Embrace surprise and delight
Increase compliance	Ask why and why not
Value accuracy	Value lessons from failure
Eliminate downside risk	Create opportunity

If you want to practice becoming more open to surprises, a great way to start is to pick one of the innovation mindsets that you find hardest to embrace and work to tackle problems while holding it in mind. It sounds tricky, but it can often be as straightforward as asking yourself "How would I behave differently if I was working to value the right question instead of the right answer?" or "How might I work on creating opportunity instead of focusing entirely on eliminating downside risk?"

When we work to embrace new mindsets, the range of behaviors we contemplate is expanded and changed. We are able to see beyond our typical toolbox—to recognize that the wrench we typically reach for may not be the right fit for the problem we are facing, and to rummage around for something that might give us more purchase. In the end, we may end up surprising ourselves—which is far and away the most enjoyable type of surprise.

FORTUNATELY, UNFORTUNATELY

There's an improv game called Fortunately, Unfortunately that works like this: The first person kicks it off by saying "Fortunately" and then adding a seemingly positive situation, such as "Fortunately, I inherited a bar of gold from my dear departed grandfather." The next person then has to build on the story but take it in the opposite direction: "Unfortunately, I'm deathly allergic to gold, and attempting to take it to the bank left me with a severe skin condition." The game continues with each person ping-ponging back and forth and adding their positive or negative contribution to the story.

Beyond being a solid party game, there is a deeper message behind Fortunately, Unfortunately: it reminds us that not only is the future unknown and unknowable, but so is how the present will appear from the future. One only has to look at the life stories of some people who have won massive sums of money in the lottery to see how something that initially seems to be good fortune can in retrospect be perceived as a tragedy. The same is true for pressure over the long haul. When we look back, will we see our current period of pressure as a difficult but essential crucible that led to better things, or as a needless period of suffering that could have been avoided? It's impossible to know until we arrive at the future.

Christine Sinclair is widely regarded as one of the best soccer players of all time. She is the all-time leader in international goals in women's soccer, a mark she achieved when she passed Abby Wambach in February 2020. She's a perennial all-star with the Portland Thorns, the captain of Canada's National Team, and an

Olympic silver medalist. And when she played in the 2011 World Cup, she was devastated.

"We headed into that tournament as the favorites to possibly win the thing—and we just unraveled," she recalled as we chatted in Ottawa seven years later. Canada lost 2–1 to the Germans to open the tournament, and then suffered a humiliating 4–0 loss to France that eliminated them. After being knocked out, they lost 1–0 to 27th-ranked Nigeria and flew home having finished dead last. "Players on the team were questioning 'Why am I even playing?'" said Sinclair. "We embarrassed ourselves, embarrassed the country, our coach quit . . ." An iconic photo of Sinclair following the loss to France shows her sitting on the turf, despondent after the game, jersey pulled up over her face, sobbing on the field.

A short while later in our interview, I asked a question that seemed related—at least to me: "What's the biggest setback you've ever encountered? And how did you overcome it?" The question seemed to stump Sinclair. "Setbacks? What are those?" she replied. I persevered: "What about the story you just told about finishing dead last at a World Cup—feeling humiliated, like you had let the country down?" This was met with a quick shake of the head. "No one from that team quit; we rallied around the defeats that we suffered. We weren't going to let that tournament define us." That loss, Sinclair explained, was the catalyst for the team to go on and win Canada's first-ever Olympic medal in soccer the following year in London. It certainly wasn't a setback.

Unfortunately, fortunately.

I asked Johann Koss, whom we met in Chapter 5, the same question about his greatest setback. As with Sinclair, the question was followed by 10 to 15 seconds of silence as he tried to process it. Finally, he volunteered, "I know there were times in my life when I felt really bad, but whether they were setbacks or not, I'm not sure. It's hard to say, because something good always came out of it."

Just because you feel bad doesn't mean it's a setback. Just because you feel happy doesn't mean it's a victory. In the present, every moment is suspended in perfect uncertainty—it exists simultaneously as a potential triumph and a potential tragedy. Which of these it actually is can only be revealed to us in the fullness of time.

The inherent uncertainty of both the future and how the present will look from the future means there is no wrong answer: in the moment, we are equally right whether we choose to see what we are experiencing as a setback or as a challenge we can rise to, and we get to decide what we choose to believe about the future. One of the big misconceptions about optimism is that it asks people to delude themselves—that the act of reframing is about trying to convince ourselves that a negative situation is actually positive. In fact, reframing has nothing to do with selling ourselves a false bill of goods; it's about surrendering to the reality that we cannot predict the future, and about choosing to see *all* of what might be true.

WHAT DOES "THINGS WILL WORK OUT" ACTUALLY MEAN?

In the seminal book *Good to Great*, Jim Collins recounts the story of James Stockdale, a naval officer who was taken prisoner at the start of the Vietnam War. Held captive for more than seven years, he was beaten, tortured, and held alone in a three- by nine-foot cell with a light bulb permanently illuminated, with no sense of when or even if he would be released. And yet, despite all these horrors, at the end of the war he emerged unbroken, going on to become an admiral in the US Navy and eventually to run for vice president in 1992.

When Stockdale talked about how he made it through that intense crucible, both in *Good to Great* and in his remarkable book *Courage Under Fire*, he would point to three main things. First, he ruthlessly separated what he could control from what he couldn't and focused on what was in his control—a core lesson from Chapter 7. Second, he and his fellow captives devised a system of communication. By tapping on their cell walls, they were able to break the immense feeling of loneliness and isolation that accompanied their long periods of solitary confinement, soothing each other after periods of torture and dispensing forgiveness and compassion to those who were wracked by having spilled secrets under physical duress. Social support was crucial. Finally, he held an unshakeable belief that things would work out in the end. "I never lost faith in the end of the story, I never doubted not only that I would get out, but also that I would prevail in the end," he said. But there was a vital qualification to this faith in the future. When Collins asked Stockdale about what characterized people who didn't make it out, Stockdale replied: "The optimists. Oh, they were the ones who said, 'We're going to be out by Christmas.' And then Christmas would come, and Christmas would go. Then they'd say, 'We're going to be out by Easter.' And then Easter would come, and Easter would go. . . . And they died of a broken heart."

Collins called this the "Stockdale paradox," which Admiral Stockdale summarized as an ability to have the discipline to "confront the most brutal facts of your reality"—warts and all—while never losing "faith that you will prevail in the end."

Believing that things will work out in the end does not mean holding an irrational conviction that everything will go smoothly or that the journey will be easy. It means recognizing that the road may be long, hard, messy, and difficult, but in the end, things will work out as they should. Stockdale used the words "faith that you will prevail in the end." I just used the phrase "work out as they should." Victor Frankl, who shared circumstances similar to Stockdale's, talked about firmly holding a mental image of himself educating students about the horrors of the Holocaust after the war in order to find meaning in the suffering he was enduring. While we all used different words—"prevail," "work out," "find meaning"—these concepts are all united in that they suggest viewing the future with hope rather than fear.

The opposite view is a sense that, if the future is uncertain, perhaps it is best to not expect too much, lest we get disappointed. My Scottish grandmother, Dorothy, was firmly of this belief. I remember, on a beautiful spring day many years ago, my dad remarking on how nice a day it was, within earshot of my grandmother. "We'll pay for it later," she assured him. Of course, this mindset has deep roots—families who have survived generations of hardship tend to expect that misfortune is always close by, and they have lots of data to support their view. It becomes a self-reinforcing cycle.

Holding on to hope rather than fear requires recognizing that there are many ways in which things can work out. Sometimes, as in Christine Sinclair's case, "working out" means a Hollywood-worthy redemptive moment of Olympic triumph. More frequently, however, things work out in a way that isn't quite as neat and tidy. Stockdale emerged from Vietnam mentally unbroken but with permanently debilitating injuries that made it tough for him to walk. In part due to his physical issues and hearing loss, he floundered as a vice-presidential candidate and, for a brief period, became a punchline on *Saturday Night Live* as the caricature of a "doddering old man." Life can be patently unfair.

So what does "work out" truly mean? Well, as a start, here are some examples I've heard in my interviews:

- I learned something new that was incredibly useful later on.
- I gained better insight into my own motivations and behaviors.
- I discovered an inner strength that I did not fully appreciate.
- I built confidence in my abilities.
- I built stronger connections to people around me.
- I was forced to recognize that the path I was on wasn't what I truly wanted.

The plurality of this list ties together a number of the concepts in this chapter. It reinforces Stockdale's concept of prevailing, which to him was not just about securing release from hell but about what he would take from the experience—how he would see it as a defining moment. But it also reflects Melissa Quinn's insight into remaining open to surprises—in this case not just along the path to the destination, but on the nature of the destination itself. How things work out may not fit with the picture in our mind's eye, but at the end of the day we never traverse a period of great uncertainty without gaining something.

When we hold to a belief that things will work out while remaining open to what form the victory will take, then we are truly embracing all of what is true.

BELIEF ≠ COMPLACENCY

Holding a patient faith that things will work out in the end does not mean believing that there is no reason to act or that effort is not required.

In the Buddhist school of thought, both attachment and resistance can lead to suffering. By becoming attached to the things that we love or value, we begin to fear their loss and start to lose our ability to enjoy them in the moment. In the midst of a wonderful night out with friends, if I start to realize that it's getting late and I need to go home soon, my joy is now tempered with a sadness that it will soon end. Similarly, when we try to push away the things that cause us pain, we end up multiplying their impact. As my friend Maria Gonzalez writes in her remarkable book *Mindful Leadership*, "Pain is inevitable. This isn't a pessimistic view; it's just the reality of life. *Suffering*, on the other hand, is optional. Suffering occurs when you resist . . . when you resist, not only do you suffer but you also perpetuate the suffering. The reality is that what you resist persists."

When Buddhism—or, similarly, stoicism—comes under fire, it tends to be because people read Buddhists' commitment to acceptance as an abdication of action. Simply accepting the good and the bad without either becoming attached or pushing away can seem like a recipe for a rudderless life, like we simply adjust and adapt to whatever may come—*que será, será*—rather than trying to impact our circumstances. And yet nothing could be further from the truth.

Dr. Marjorie Dixon was no stranger to pressure. As a first-generation Jamaican Canadian, she had been raised to believe that anything was possible but not to underestimate the work that would be required. "My parents always told me that [Canada] will do a lot for you. If you do right by it, give back, and work hard, you can do anything you want to do."

After completing medical school and residency, Dixon set up a fertility practice with a partner. It was a modest operation: Dixon, her partner, and a handful of staff. But she had much bigger plans: "I felt like complacency was part of the industry of women's health and fertility, and I just felt like women were being short-changed. And I was like 'I'm a revolutionary anti-misogynist from Planet Venus, and I am going to come in and revolutionize this industry and be the best.'"

Not one to stand still, she started to move from idea to action, sketching out a bold plan for a large women's health and fertility center with a state-of-the-art on-site in vitro fertility (IVF) lab that would set a new standard in Canada. "We were building a spaceship," she says.

Right from the start, the pressure was intense. While continuing to treat patients, Dixon began navigating what it would mean to go from running a small center to designing and building a large clinic with 24 staff members. First of all, there was the financial risk: "I was the driving force financially in it and had to leverage myself up to my kidneys with RBC. And so I didn't sleep." Just to secure the new space required a credit note against a commitment of more than $50,000 per month in rent.

Then, her business partner pulled out of their shareholder agreement. Feeling that the venture was too risky, she agreed to move her patients over, but she would no longer put any money into the business.

"I remember where I was sitting. I remember what I felt. It was almost physical, like someone punched me in the gut." The drop in funds from her partner ramped up the financial pressure, forcing Dixon to be even more aggressive in what she herself was committing to the endeavor.

Then, five months before the targeted opening date, the clinic encountered significant construction delays. Everyone involved realized that the original timeline was not feasible; they needed to push the opening back. Her current landlord, sensing an opportunity, sent her a letter stating that her rent was increasing by $50,000 a month.

"I remember thinking, *I have been through so much*—medical school, residency, fellowship, moving to different countries, finding a partner, having children, owning two houses in the middle of the financial crisis in 2009—all of those things felt like nothing in comparison." The people close to her started to get concerned: "My friends and family genuinely thought I was just fully off my rocker and were really worried about being able to sustain with everything that stood on my shoulders."

Faced with mounting crises, Dixon did what she always did: she got resourceful. "They called me Pollyanna as a fellow because I always felt like I could figure it out. 'It's okay. Patient's bleeding out. I got this. It's okay. I can come up with a solution.'"

Her solutions started to work. With huge effort, the clinic's ultrasound license had come through in the midst of her challenges, something that helped alleviate the financial risk. She hired a lawyer to push back on her predatory landlord. "I didn't know lawyers existed in so many disciplines, but now I understand the utility of the lawyers," she says now, only half joking. Construction started to move again. The hits kept coming, but there was progress.

As the tide turned and things started to move ahead, another bomb dropped: with only months to go, her partner announced that she would no longer bring her patients over or participate in any way. The financial implications were huge, and their relationship deteriorated to the point where, even though they continued to work out of the same space, they communicated through lawyers. "Every month, there was another minute of me holding my breath and feeling overwhelmed, and then eventually saying, *Okay, I'm going to survive this; I'll survive this.*"

Finally, three months after the original opening date, and frustrated with the delays, Dixon called a meeting with the building company. "I said, 'The moving truck is coming Monday, come hell or high water. You're going to have to work through weekends, work in the evenings—I actually don't care how you do it, but you're going to get it set because this is the only way you're going to get paid for your job.' The bluff worked and the builders agreed to the new deadline."

The day arrived. The moving trucks came, staff arrived, and things—well, things worked out. They finished setting up the space at 2 a.m. on Tuesday, and at 7 a.m. Anova Fertility and Reproductive Health was open for business, with patients arriving. "I had an embryology department. I had an ultrasound department. IT was wired, reception was ready, all the new computers were set up." It wasn't without its glitches, but they did it. In the end, almost unbelievably, they missed only one day of operation.

Today, the business is thriving, and embodies Dixon's original mission of building a next-generation, fully inclusive, and innovative space for fertility and reproductive care. Looking back on that incredible year and a half, Dixon reflects: "I live a supercharged life. I have pushed to the limits and beyond and survived it. I recognize that it's like a roller-coaster. What goes down eventually does come up. Like a pendulum. It swings; it'll swing back to the other side. This too shall pass. And when you get to the other side, you learn lessons that will serve to inform you on your next challenge."

It's not that she doesn't fear failure. Quite the opposite, in fact: "Failure is always an option. It's always there. It's right behind. The wind beneath my wings is that failure, actually—I'm driven by my adversity to catastrophic failure. But there is a solution to every problem that presents itself. Often, it's not the solution you want or that you might've come up with in the first iteration, but eventually, when you come up on the other end, you're like 'Go figure that that was going to be the way this was going to turn out!' I can't always predict it. I can't. I can't always predict it."

This summation from Dr. Dixon gets at the heart of resolving the tension between acceptance and giving up. Ultimately, resilience over the long haul in the face of uncertainty is rooted in a deep-seated belief that if you devote yourself fully to the cause and work tirelessly to control the things you can control, things will work out—even if they work out a little differently than you expected.

THE LIMITS OF CONTROL

Depending on your predisposition, you may find one side of the uncertainty paradox a little easier to hold than the other. Some who are a little more pessimistic (or realistic, as they would have you believe) have no trouble accepting that the future is unknown and unknowable but find it difficult to hold to a belief that things will work out. Others have the opposite challenge: they firmly believe that the future is within their control and that things will work out exactly as diagrammed if they apply enough effort. A common theme in my interviews was the determination to exert control through immense personal effort before ultimately relenting by coming to a place of acceptance. It's a challenge that disproportionately affects high performers, who have often experienced tremendous success when they have taken control in the past.

Years before Rick Hansen embarked on his Man in Motion World Tour, he was a teenager struggling with a life he had not expected and did not accept. Told by doctors that he would never walk again, he refused to believe it. "The first phase was absolute bitter denial. I'll find a way to walk again. I'm determined. I've been able to overcome so many obstacles. I'll just focus every day. Literally every single day, and almost every waking moment, I sat there visualizing my toes moving and the ability to walk again. I used every athletic trick in the book. I prayed to God. I visualized. I worked my butt off, did everything. I even looked for just little snippets of hope somewhere that would come from a prognosis, or a statement, or a word coming out of a doctor's mouth, or a nurse, or a physio—anything that I could do to believe that they were wrong and that I was going to return to the life that I once had." At the end of the day, none of it worked. "Every part of my character was dedicated to grinding it out and trying to take control of the situation, to use positive thinking, use effort and determination, and it just didn't seem to pay off."

In the end, Rick's life is a testament to things working out in a different way than expected. He couldn't control the future, and attempting to do so simply created a longer and more painful road to acceptance, but ultimately he arrived and was able to accomplish things that would have been impossible without going through the ordeal.

The future is unknowable.

How the present will look from the future is unknowable.

It will work out in the end.

CHAPTER 8

SIMPLIFY

VOLUME IN PEAK
PRESSURE MOMENTS

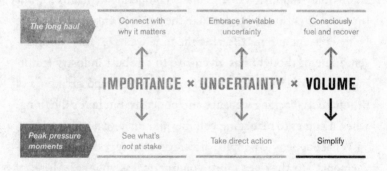

I n the immediate lead-up to our peak pressure moments, volume can be overwhelming. Before a big sales presentation, when you desperately need to be prepping and rehearsing, your boss's boss's boss casually drops in to see "how things are going" and asks if you can join a management meeting to provide a quick update. In our personal world, it often seems like our peak pressure moments are accompanied by a cascade of poorly timed volume. Our move to a new house manages to per-fectly sync with our car breaking down, our kid getting sick, and the air conditioning going on the fritz. There is a reason we say "When it rains, it pours."

In peak pressure moments, volume collides with biological reality. When pressure mounts, our ability to pay attention to multiple inputs diminishes, our attentional focus narrows, and even a normal level of volume can start to feel overwhelming and distracting. We begin to feel like we are missing things or letting balls drop. The worry that we are neglecting our responsibilities adds to our pressure.

In the face of relentless volume, time management seems like an obvious response. With so many competing demands for our time and attention, it can feel like the key is to ensure that we are being efficient and maximizing the time we have. This common-sense line of thought has given rise to a robust industry featur-ing books like David Allen's *Getting Things Done* and a plethora of productivity-hacking websites and podcasts. But here's the thing: when it comes to managing volume, *time management is a trap*.

What happens to people who are incredibly good at time man-agement? Do they get more volume or less volume? More, of course. More responsibility. More tasks. More direct reports. In short, time-management techniques may be helpful for your pro-ductivity and your career, but they don't alleviate pressure, they add to it.

Focusing on time management is a great way to add volume. The reality is that we need to do the exact opposite.

THE SOLUTION TO VOLUME: SIMPLIFY

When pressure is intense and volume is part of the reason, our number one imperative is to eliminate: to engage in a process of radical simplification that allows us to focus on what matters in the moment.

At age 25, Ben Cowan-Dewar had spent four years assembling 13 parcels of land on the coast of Cape Breton, a gorgeous island in the Atlantic, to build what he was convinced would be one of the best golf courses in the world. Against all odds, he had secured the backing of Mike Keiser, one of the most successful golf developers in the world. And then the 2008 financial crisis hit and all construction on new courses stopped. "Mike phoned me and said, 'We can't move forward with the project,'" remembers Cowan-Dewar. Faced with the prospect of financial ruin for his young family, who had moved from Toronto to Cape Breton, built a new house, and staked their future on the course, Ben moved to aggressively simplify. "We were budgeted to spend about $3 million that year, and I pitched a plan of spending $305,000. I think Mike's line was 'So, you've been sitting in Canada all winter and you've come up with a number that is so laughably low, I have to keep going.'" The simplification worked, construction continued, and Cabot Links and Cabot Cliffs are now both among the world's best courses, with Cliffs ranked in the top 10 globally.

When swimmer Martha McCabe was preparing for her first Olympic Trials in 2012, she started realizing that the volume of outreach from her friends, her family, and the media was becoming a source of pressure for her. Her solution? She deleted all of her social media apps and got a new SIM card for her phone, with a different phone number that she gave out to only a tight inner circle. It's instructive to note that McCabe's solution in the face of pressure wasn't to figure out how to be more efficient so that she could slot in time for the demands from media, family, friends, and well-wishers, it was to act to dramatically to simplify her life, taking concrete steps to eliminate as much volume and as many distractions as she could.

This imperative to simplify, or focus, is advice that can be seen consistently across high-performing environments. Legendary Athletics Ontario coach Andy Higgins, who coached both David Steen and Michael Smith to Olympic medals in decathlon, distributed a sheet entitled "General Thoughts on Training" to all new athletes joining his program. It contained this passage:

> You can do two things well, there are three:
>   1. school or job;
>   2. athletics;
>   3. relationships/social life.
>
> You have to choose. So long as you are clear on your priorities and have consciously made the choice, no one emphasis is any better than another. TO TRAIN IN THIS GROUP, ATHLETICS MUST BE ONE OF THE PRIORITIES.

Similarly, Randi Zuckerberg, Facebook's former head of marketing (and Mark's sister) summed up her perspective on focus when she talked about the "entrepreneur's dilemma":

Randi Zuckerberg ✔
@randizuckerberg

The entrepreneur's dilemma:

Maintaining friendships. Building a great company. Spending time w/family. Staying fit. Getting sleep.

Pick 3.

♡ 1,606   2:43 AM - Dec 9, 2011   ⓘ

💬 2,751 people are talking about this   ›

Whether you believe either of these *specific* formulas—and I'm not so sure I do—what is consistent between them is the reality that we all need to determine what volume we want to embrace and what needs to be off-loaded or ignored so we can focus on what matters most.

In Third Factor's programs on resilience, we talk about the concept of foreground and background. There are numerous areas in our lives we can choose to focus on. Higgins identified work or school, social life, and athletics in his list. Zuckerberg focused on sleep, fitness, work, friends, and family. I would add practicing your faith, engaging in recreation or hobbies, traveling, giving back, and pursuing personal development. During different periods of your life, different priorities will be in the foreground for you. If you want to train in Higgins's gym, athletics will need to be in the foreground for that period of time. As we age, health tends to increasingly come to the foreground as a conscious focus, rather than a background concern that we monitor in service of performance in other areas. The key is to ensure that you are being deliberate about what you keep in your foreground and are not simply being battered by the day to day.

When personal productivity expert Chris Bailey turned in the manuscript for his second book, the terrific *Hyperfocus*, he sent out a blog post that really resonated with me based on what I've heard from other high performers. He talked about a morning spent cleaning his office after finishing the book—wiping the dust off his desk and the photos in his office: "This made me reflect on what other things had accumulated 'dust' while I was writing the book. Obviously, dust had accumulated on my relationships with the people in the frames. Some dust had also accumulated on a few of my other friendships during this time. Dust had even accumulated on this blog." He went on to note: "In thinking a bit more about the dust that had accumulated, another thought crossed my mind: *the costs of writing the book were easily worth it*. Every single decision has costs—including over-investing in one area of your life." He talks about this notion of over-investing as "tilting." Both dust and the word "tilting" are terrific metaphors for the central notion of simplifying in times of peak pressure. When we're pursuing something intensely important to us, our ability to tilt toward that and simplify the rest is vital.

TIDYING UP PRESSURE

Marie Kondo is an unlikely global superstar. From a young age, she was obsessed with cleaning up, often staying behind to organize the bookshelves in her classroom while other students at her school in Tokyo were off at gym class. A passion for organizing is not a typical path to fame and fortune, but in 2015 she published *The Life-Changing Magic of Tidying Up*, which became a smash hit that made her the globe's de facto guru on tidying. This was followed by the Netflix series *Tidying Up with Marie Kondo*, which catapulted her—and her KonMari Method of tidying—into broad public consciousness.

The KonMari Method is anchored in an epiphany that Kondo had early in life. She described it to the newspaper *The Australian* as follows: "I was obsessed with what I could throw away. One day, I had a kind of nervous breakdown and fainted. I was unconscious for two hours. When I came to, I heard a mysterious voice, like some god of tidying telling me to look at my things more closely. And I realized my mistake: I was only looking for things to throw out. What I should be doing is finding the things I want to keep. Identifying the things that make you happy: that is the work of tidying."

Even if you haven't read Kondo's books, you may be familiar with the core of the KonMari Method that this epiphany triggered. Kondo recommends that you hold each of your possessions in your hands and ask, "Does this spark joy?" If the item brings joy to your life, keep it. If not, it can go.

The KonMari Method for tidying up our physical environment is a wonderful source of inspiration for what we need to do to tidy up the volume in our lives that creates pressure. Imagine if Kondo's solution to clutter was simply to build a bigger closet. That's the premise of time management: let's make space for everything. Simplifying means that, instead, we take a look at the volume we are facing and ask ourselves what we want to keep.

So how do we decide what to keep? We can't simply use Kondo's question about joy. As we've discussed, the pressure we are facing won't often bring us joy. Instead, let's return to some of the goals we've identified when it comes to navigating pressure:

- **Goal 1: To perform to my potential.** This goal is the core imperative in peak pressure moments.
- **Goal 2: To grow in ways that matter to me.** As we saw in Chapter 4, growth is a big part of what gives meaning to pressure. When pressure helps us get better, we feel like it matters.
- **Goal 3: To emerge without regret.** A big part of facing pressure over the long haul is ensuring that we come out of it with a sense of satisfaction that we did what we could to rise to the challenge and acquitted ourselves honorably.

Embedded in these goals are a few key questions that can help us audit the volume in our lives in the lead-up to peak pressure moments. As Kondo recommends, "hold" each piece of the volume you are facing in mind and ask yourself three questions: Will this help me grow? Does this help or hurt my performance? Will eliminating this lead to regret?

WILL THIS HELP ME GROW?

This question gets to the heart of peak pressure by taking a look at what types of peak pressure moments we choose to face. In the lead-up to a peak pressure moment, the reflexive imperative often isn't to clear away the ancillary sources of pressure, it's to abandon ship entirely. In the same way that our minds and bodies often work against us in the middle of a hard workout, begging us to quit a few minutes early just to make the pain stop, we often feel an overwhelming urge to make the discomfort of a peak pressure moment go away by choosing to opt out. In the middle of a hard workout, what keeps us pushing is a clear sense that it is good for us—it will make us stronger, better, faster.

You will want to ask this question of yourself honestly. If you are facing peak pressure and it is not in some way linked to growth, it can feel debilitating. If, over the long haul, you continue to face peak pressure moments that you can't link to growth, it's time to take a hard look at what you're "keeping in your closet."

This question has helped me gain great clarity on the peak pressure moments I take on in my life. A couple of years ago I had an epiphany that the work I was doing to help organizations draft their strategic plans was not helping me grow in ways that mattered to me. It was a source of constant pressure, and something that I was taking on because it was work I knew how to do, but it ultimately wasn't helping me get any better. Speaking to large groups of people was actually *more* stressful to me, but it was far more closely linked to my growth. One stayed in the closet, the other got the boot.

If you are an optimist, it can be tempting to answer yes to this question for every responsibility that's creating pressure in your life. Everything is a growth opportunity because, at the very least, it will teach you how to tolerate discomfort, navigate high levels of pressure, or build perseverance. This attitude is hugely helpful when facing the long haul of pressure that we cannot control or tame, but it can be counterproductive when we are looking for places to simplify in the face of peak pressure. Try to temporarily put on your pessimist hat when asking yourself this question.

DOES THIS HELP OR HURT MY PERFORMANCE?

This question is the key filter for the other sources of pressure that surround your peak pressure moments. If, after answering the previous question, you are committed to facing your peak pressure moment, you will want to audit all the other volume in your life with this one. Early on, Martha McCabe realized that giving a wide group of friends, family, and supporters access to her was creating a source of pressure that wasn't going to assist her performance in any way. That realization made it an easy item to jettison.

Answering this question is a great way to audit the peripheral pressure that can surround peak pressure moments. People who excel in incredibly high-pressure situations are rigorous about eliminating the sources of pressure that are ancillary to performance.

WILL ELIMINATING THIS LEAD TO REGRET?

There are some sources of pressure that won't help us perform and aren't connected to the ways in which we are looking to grow, but, ultimately, must still be endured because to abandon them would be to consign ourselves to regret down the road. In particular, for peak pressure moments that are thrust upon us rather than chosen—illness, the breakdown of a relationship, natural disasters, and so on—our desire to opt out and disconnect has the potential to dramatically impact how we view our life in the future. I know of several people who carry significant regret because they made end-of-life choices for loved ones that, in retrospect, they view as decisions made simply to eliminate pressure from their own lives.

More pragmatically, doing your taxes in the midst of the lead-up to a big presentation or exam may not benefit either your personal growth or your performance, but abandoning the task could lead to significant regret years later, from federal prison.

So what does tidying up pressure look like in reality? Let's apply it to a hypothetical peak pressure situation. In this case, we'll use a grad student who is heading toward a defense of his thesis and, at the same time, is dealing with a variety of other real-world stressors. He has a job at a restaurant, has teaching assistant responsibilities as part of his degree, has offered to help a friend move, and has joined the committee that is planning the end-of-year social. As the thesis defense becomes more imminent, he starts to realize that he is feeling immense pressure from carrying all of these obligations, and that trying to do them all simultaneously may result in him not performing well.

Figure 7 is what a hypothetical audit of his situation could look like. Based on this audit there are two obvious outcomes: recommitting to the thesis defense and cutting the end-of-year social. That's the easy stuff. Now he's got three things remaining: the job, the TA responsibilities, and helping a friend move. Only one of them is linked to growth, and all are distractions from performance. He needs to keep the job—it's necessary for rent. But what about the TA responsibilities and helping a friend move? If

WILL THIS . . .	PEAK PRESSURE:	OTHER VOLUME:			
	Defending my thesis	Job at restaurant	TA responsibilities	Helping friend move	Planning end-of-year social
HELP ME GROW?	*Yes, absolutely. Key to my path forward.*	*No*	*Yes, somewhat*	*No*	*No*
HELP OR HURT MY PERFORMANCE?		*Hurt*	*Hurt*	*Hurt*	*Hurt*
LEAD TO REGRET IF I ABANDON IT?		*Yes, necessary for rent*	*Minimal*	*Somewhat: I'll feel bad*	*No: lots of other committee members*

FIGURE 7: *Hypothetical audit of peak pressure*

he keeps the TA responsibilities and jettisons helping the friend move, he is optimizing for his own growth but possibly letting his friend down, which will lead to regret. Not life-altering regret, but regret nonetheless. If he opts out of his TA responsibilities and helps his friend, he has the opposite challenge.

There are no black-and-white answers in these types of situations, and both personal growth and contribution to others can give meaning to pressure, as we discussed in Chapter 4. However, he likely should jettison both. He can find a friend who isn't facing a thesis defense to replace him as the helpful mover, minimizing his feeling that he's letting his friend down, and, with apologies to the professor, park his TA responsibilities until the thesis defense is over. Neither of these obligations is significantly contributing to his growth, and neither will lead to lasting regret if abandoned, but both are distracting him from performing.

Nailing the moments that are deeply important to you and significantly connected to your growth is vital—they have the potential to bend the arc of your journey for better or worse. Simplifying to minimize the surrounding volume isn't always easy, but it is worth it.

SIMPLIFY HOW?

Conceptually, simplifying makes sense, but practically, in the face of peak pressure, it can be challenging to do. In the age of social media, relying on willpower alone to shut out distractions is a losing bet. You're in a tug-of-war with an unseen and massive foe—thousands of our generation's best minds working tirelessly to figure out how to get your attention by exploiting weaknesses in the human brain.

In a remarkable interview in 2017, Facebook's founding president, Sean Parker, talked about how he had become "something of a conscientious objector" to social media. He went on to talk about what had led him to that position: "The thought process that went into building these [social media] applications, Facebook being the first of them . . . was all about: 'How do we consume as much of your time and conscious attention as possible?' And that means that we need to sort of give you a little dopamine hit every once in a while, because someone liked or commented on a photo or a post or whatever. And that's going to get you to contribute more content, and that's going to get you more likes and comments." As Parker notes, "It's a social-validation feedback loop . . . exactly the kind of thing that a hacker like myself would come up with, because you're exploiting a vulnerability in human psychology."

Consider how many apps you have on your phone. Each of those apps has a team of people working on exactly the same problem: How do we get users to spend more time in the app? When a service is free, your attention is the inventory. That's what they are selling to advertisers. So, whether it's the dopamine hit of likes and comments, a notification that shades down just-so in your peripheral vision, or a rhythmic tap of vibrations from your phone or watch, all of it is precisely calibrated to tap into the elements of the human psyche that are vulnerable to distraction.

Structural simplification is by far the most effective way to shut out distractions. When Martha McCabe got a new SIM card for her phone leading up to Olympic trials, she didn't have to will herself to ignore calls, texts, and notifications; she put a structural firewall in place that allowed her to focus her willpower where it would be most useful: her training and preparation.

My most productive periods are spent on airplanes. Even when there is Wi-Fi, it tends to be slow enough and expensive enough that I end up operating in distraction-free mode. Unable to get notifications, receive new email, or read the news, I can stay focused on a single task with unbelievable ease (something that is a great challenge for me day to day). Without the forced simplification provided by airplanes, it's doubtful that this book would exist!

Now, we can't hop on a plane any time we need to simplify, and most of us aren't willing to go as far as McCabe did and ignore everything—at least over the long haul. So another way we can effectively use structure to simplify is to deal in absolutes. In his seminal *Harvard Business Review* article "How Will You Measure Your Life?" legendary Harvard Business School professor Clayton Christensen talked eloquently about the value of holding to absolute principles. At Oxford University, Clay was an unusual combination of a Rhodes Scholar and the six-foot-five starting center of the school's basketball team. After working hard and finishing the regular season undefeated, the team made it to the semifinals of the National Championships. But there was a problem: the game was on a Sunday and Clay, a deeply religious man, had made a commitment to himself and God that he would not play on Sundays.

His coach and teammates were incredulous. They implored him to play; they reminded him that these were exceptional circumstances—surely he could make an exception for such an important game. But after prayer and quiet contemplation, Clay decided to hold to his principles. He wrote: "Resisting the temptation whose logic was 'In this extenuating circumstance, just this once, it's OK' has proven to be one of the most important decisions of my life. Why? My life has been one unending stream of extenuating circumstances. Had I crossed the line that one time, I would have done it over and over in the years that followed." In the end, "The lesson I learned from this is that it's easier to hold to your principles 100% of the time than it is to hold to them 98% of the time."

This isn't just true when it comes to religious convictions or other moral matters: the research is clear that in almost any area it requires less willpower to stick to absolute rules. When we make exceptions, it begins to create pressure. In weight management, for example, it is much more effective to say "I won't eat after 7 p.m." than it is to say "I'll limit my snacking after 7 p.m." One creates the pressure of additional decisions; the other simply shuts the door.

Podcaster and human performance expert Tim Ferriss talks about structural simplification as finding "the one decision that removes 100 decisions." For Tim, who was receiving multiple books a day with requests for a review or blurb, simplification meant deciding to read *no* new books in 2020. Steve Jobs famously decided to wear the same thing every day to remove the decision fatigue of choosing an outfit every morning. One constant source of pressure in my household is the relentless requests from my kids for iPad, Netflix, and Minecraft time. After months of trying to work within a system of "reasonable limits"—in which each of the requests for a device required my wife and me to consult on whether we should allow it, and ultimately led to the kind of high-stakes, high-emotion bartering and negotiation discussions that only your own children can deliver—we finally created a simple and absolute rule: screens are available only while dinner is being prepared. This simple decision has eliminated close to 50 decisions a week, along with a ton of frustration.

In our day-to-day lives, setting clear, absolute principles is one of the most effective ways to simplify and combat volume over the long haul.

CHAPTER 9

SLEEP AND OTHER INCONVENIENT NECESSITIES

VOLUME OVER THE LONG HAUL

The long haul | Connect with why it matters | Embrace inevitable uncertainty | Consciously fuel and recover

IMPORTANCE × UNCERTAINTY × VOLUME

Peak pressure moments | See what's *not* at stake | Take direct action | Simplify

hil Wilkins was on the road. As the person in charge of building out a new business unit for a financial technology start-up that was looking to grow revenue from $5 million to $100 million in a year and a half, he had been living out of a suitcase for months. "I was on the road three to four days a week, going from Toronto to St. Louis to Denver to Austin to San Francisco for single meetings," he remembers. He'd joined knowing what he was in for: "They said, 'Here's a blank page. Whatever you need, just build it all into a business case as to why you need it, when you need it, and how much you need.' So it was really starting from the ground up with the team saying, 'We know nothing about this market, we think there's an opportunity there, go nuts.'"

All the same, it was tough—not just on Wilkins, but on his family as well. When he took the job, he had a two-year-old, and twins on the way. Over the next 18 months, he missed his twins' first words, their first steps, and his daughter's first day of preschool.

This road trip was different, though. After putting in a 20-hour day of travel and client meetings, Wilkins was exhausted. He was driving to another meeting in Philadelphia when he had a seizure behind the wheel that led to a serious accident. He woke up in an ambulance. "I didn't know where I was, didn't know what had happened. I was with someone on my team. It was pretty terrifying." After being treated in the hospital, he was diagnosed with epilepsy—something that had never presented before—and told that diet and sleep were big contributors to the prevalence of seizures. He left in a wheelchair, with strict instructions regarding diet, rest, and recovery.

I met Wilkins a couple of months later, when his company brought my firm in to do resilience training—in no small part due to some soul searching triggered by the accident. He remained banged up, having just progressed past walking with a cane after several weeks in the wheelchair. Shortly after our meeting he told me that he wanted his accident to be a lesson for others. Wilkins had figured a lack of sleep was one of the things that came with his high-stakes, high-pressure job. He averaged five hours of sleep a night. "With the lack of eating right, all the travel, probably the emotional toll, it sort of really all came to a head. My body broke down."

The accident forced Wilkins to confront the biological realities of sleep, nutrition, and resilience. "Looking back now, I always knew it was too much, I needed to slow down. But the drive to do what I signed up for kept me going." Following the accident, Wilkins took a hard look at what he valued most in his life and made a conscious choice to prioritize rest and recovery. "You start asking all of these questions. Am I prioritizing the right things?" He left his computer at work, he put his phone in a box when he got home, and he tried to get seven hours of sleep a night. He also implemented changes for his team. Emails sent after 5:30 p.m. could not be answered until the following morning. "It was a message of 'Take a break'—don't think that when you go on vacation you need to work. You can still hold yourself to a high standard without sacrificing everything," he says. One of the things that surprised him most was that carving out rest and recovery time didn't impact the team's productivity at all. "You had this feeling of always having to be responsive. And realistically, at the end of the day, nothing changed [when we started setting boundaries]. The only thing that changed is that I felt I was a little more present at home."

One other thing did change: the culture of the company. Prior to the accident, Wilkins notes, "They had used me as this model of someone coming in and being willing to make sacrifices for the betterment of the company and to achieve things. That was kind of what was celebrated. Then you fast-forward to me coming back into the office and people seeing me with a cane. This sort of invincibility cloak disappears, and the company really starts looking internally for themselves. I have to give credit to the entire executive team, who said, 'Holy crap. This can't happen.'" Beyond offering resilience training, the company began a dialogue around how to balance the drive for results and growth with building a workplace that is sustainable over the long haul.

"So," I asked Wilkins, "do you think it's possible you would have made these changes without the accident?" He was emphatic: "No chance at all. It didn't matter what anybody said to me. Everybody—my parents, my in-laws, my friends—everybody told me before the accident, 'Phil, you've got to slow down. You've got to take a break. You're missing things. Is this all worth it?' My response to everybody was 'Shut up and leave me alone.'"

Simply put, you cannot remain mentally resilient under a heavy volume load over the long haul if you don't take care of your physical platform. "Your body is a persistent messenger," my colleague Kara Stelfox likes to say. "First it knocks, then it rings the doorbell—and then it kicks down the door."

The type of catastrophic forced perspective shift Wilkins experienced thanks to his car accident is an unfortunately common denominator in the stories of hard-charging executives who have turned into advocates for balance. Through the course of my work, I've spoken with numerous people who have changed their lives in response to a heart attack, chronic pain, or the death of a colleague. But why not get there *before* the heart attack?

Here's the good news: building a physical platform that will allow you to thrive through a high-pressure period doesn't require training to qualify for the Boston Marathon or doing an Ironman triathlon. As wonderful and healthy as those goals are— and I salute you if you're pursuing them—you don't need to aim for physical perfection in order to build a solid foundation. All it requires is that you take care of the basics in three main areas: sleep, nutrition, and movement.

SLEEP: THE FOUNDATION OF THE PYRAMID

A few years back, professor Drew Dawson of Central Queensland University in Australia and Kathryn Reid, then one of Dawson's PhD students and now a professor of neurology at Northwestern University, devised an ingenious experiment to quantify the performance impact of sleep deprivation. They recruited 40 subjects, who were split evenly and placed into two parallel experiments: the first group was kept awake for 28 hours straight—from 8 in the morning to noon the following day—and the second group was asked to drink 10 to 15 grams of alcohol every 30 minutes until their blood alcohol concentration reached 0.10%. (Results aside, I am sure the first group was less than thrilled when they learned what group 2 had been up to at the end of the experiment. Talk about drawing the short straw.)

For both groups, the researchers used a computer-based test to measure cognitive performance every 30 minutes. The data was clear: the relationship between hours of wakefulness and performance tracked almost identically to the relationship between drinking and performance. As the researchers noted: "After 17 hours of sustained wakefulness cognitive psychomotor performance decreased to a level equivalent to the performance impairment observed at a blood alcohol concentration of 0.05%.

This is the prescribed level of alcohol intoxication in many Western industrialized countries." In short, once you've been awake for more than 17 hours, you have the cognitive performance of someone who is legally drunk—a strong case for getting at least 7 hours of sleep a night.

Of course, there is a significant difference between fatigue and inebriation. In the work world, we would never celebrate someone who came to work drunk ("Dave is such a terrific accountant—he's drunk every day!"), and yet we often lionize people who work themselves to exhaustion ("Dave's incredible: he answered my email at midnight, and he's the first person in the office this morning—what a hard worker"). Yet the data tell us that, from a cognitive performance standpoint, the two states are exactly the same.

Beyond performance, however, lie the significant health implications of sacrificing sleep when we are under pressure. Wilkins experienced it firsthand when he had a seizure at the wheel of his car, but it wasn't until after his accident that he was able to see the implications of too little sleep in a controlled environment. "When you're going through all of the tests with neurologists after seizures, you do a lot of EKGs where they wire your brain up and they try to give you seizures," he recalled. As part of the tests, the doctors created a variety of different scenarios to see which factors would increase the chance of seizures. One was sleep deprivation, first for a 24-hour period and then for 48 hours. Wilkins was shocked by the results: "When I did the EKGs with no sleep, it only took minutes to induce a seizure. That was a big eye-opening experience for me—it made me realize how important sleep really was."

The links between sleep and health are only beginning to be fully understood, but already we can see that they are much broader than we thought even 10 to 20 years ago. With research centers studying sleep at every major medical school globally, a broad body of research is emerging showing links between a lack of sleep and everything from cancer to diabetes to obesity. For me, having watched my grandmother slowly descend into the grip of Alzheimer's disease, perhaps the most profound discovery is the growing evidence of a link between a lack of sleep and neurodegenerative diseases. Research done out of the University of Rochester Medical Center, led by colleagues Dr. Maiken Nedergaard and Dr. Jeffrey Iliff, has shown that sleep is when the brain cleans out the waste it accumulates during the day. The process of cleaning waste from between our cells is a basic body function that is accomplished in the rest of our organs by the lymphatic system, a network of vessels that runs in parallel with our blood vessels to collect proteins, broken-down cells, bacteria, and other waste products and deposit them into our blood for removal. The challenge that Iliff and Nedergaard tackled is that the brain lacks lymphatic vessels. As Dr. Iliff notes in his widely viewed TED talk: "The brain is this intensely active organ that produces a correspondingly large amount of waste that must be efficiently cleared. And yet, it lacks lymphatic vessels, which means that the approach that the rest of the body takes to clearing away its waste won't work in the brain."

The brain's solution to this issue is ingenious. During sleep— and only during sleep—a fluid called cerebrospinal fluid is pumped along the outside of the brain's blood vessels into every nook and cranny of the brain, flushing the waste into the bloodstream. Dr. Nedergaard's work showed that this process appears to be facilitated by the neurons in the brain shrinking by up to 60% during sleep to create space for the fluid to flow. It's an approach that is unique to the brain, and perfectly suited to an organ that is densely packed with neurons and encased in a hard shell.

One of the waste products that the brain clears during sleep is a protein called amyloid-beta. It's something produced constantly in the brain. However, as Dr. Iliff notes, "In patients with Alzheimer's disease, amyloid-beta builds up and aggregates in the spaces between the brain's cells . . . and it's this buildup of amyloid-beta that's thought to be one of the key steps in the development of that terrible disease." The less we sleep, and the worse the quality of our sleep, the less time our brain has to perform its vital house-cleaning duties. And this is a debt that we pay with our cognitive health. Dr. Iliff concludes: "When it comes to cleaning the brain, it is the very health and function of the mind and body that is at stake."

A lack of sleep also affects our emotional reactivity and the degree to which we engage in worrying. This is where we can often see the most immediate impact of sleep on our ability to handle pressure. Broadly speaking, the brain has two main systems that help us process and make sense of emotion: the "hot" system and the "cold" system. At the risk of oversimplifying dramatically, the hot system is centered in the amygdala, a part of the brain that controls our immediate emotional reactions to things. When you get cut off in traffic and have an immediate flash of anger, that is your amygdala firing. It happens before you have a chance to think. The cold system is centered in the prefrontal cortex, which is the seat of what is known as executive function—your more logical self. This is the part of the brain that subsequently gets activated to prevent you from smashing into the car that just cut you off to teach that idiot a lesson. When we engage in highly reactive behavior—when we are consumed by anger and follow through with road rage—that is what's known as an amygdala hijack, in which we are operating fully off of the hot system without engaging the cold, critical-thinking part of our brain that allows us to mediate our emotions.

A lack of sleep has been shown to do two things that are counterproductive under pressure: first, the amygdala responds more strongly to negative stimuli. In fact, in a controlled study, sleep-deprived individuals showed a 60% higher magnitude of amygdala activation in response to negative stimuli than those with adequate rest. Second, the communication link between the hot and cold systems is disrupted, which makes it harder to temper our emotional responses. When we don't get enough sleep, the fire burns hotter and the phone line to the fire station is out.

Compounding the issue of increased emotional response to current events is a heightened worry about *future* events—what is known as anticipatory anxiety. Researchers at the University of California, Berkeley, showed that sleep-deprived individuals exhibited significantly higher levels of anxiety about future events than well-rested individuals. The effect of a lack of sleep on worrying was highest in those who were "worriers" to begin with.

All of these effects of insufficient sleep create a vicious cycle when we are under pressure. If a presentation goes badly at work, not only do we feel more anger, frustration, or worry than if we were rested, but we also ruminate more on the meeting we have the next day. If we have a fight with one of our kids, we have trouble falling asleep as we worry about the future and our relationship. Lack of sleep creates heightened emotion and anxiety, which in turn makes it harder to sleep.

BREAKING THE CYCLE OF
POOR SLEEP UNDER PRESSURE

When you are under pressure, especially over the long haul, you need seven to eight hours of sleep a night. If you are getting less than that, there is no other single change you can make that will increase your ability to handle pressure more than upping your amount of sleep. The research on the importance of sleep—for physical, mental, and emotional health—is overwhelming, and it just keeps on coming.

But when you're under pressure, you may experience the vicious cycle mentioned earlier. You're on edge from lack of sleep, but when you try to sleep you can't stop worrying about what happened that day or what might happen the next day. Whether it's the lead-up to an exam, a big sales presentation, or a competition at the Olympics, it's often when we are most in need of a good night's sleep that we find sleep hardest to come by.

So how do we establish positive sleep routines that will serve us well over the long haul? And how do we ensure that we are well-rested heading into the peak pressure moments we all face? While the strategies that serve these two scenarios are related, there are some differences.

GETTING SLEEP OVER THE LONG HAUL

There has been a ton of research on the healthy routines that promote consistency in sleep. If you've read an article on sleep over the past three to five years, you have likely come across a list of the things you can do in this area. Here are the ones that have consistently shown to provide the biggest bang for your buck:

- **Keep it dark, keep it cool:** Our bodies use light and heat as markers to determine when it's time to initiate the physical processes that lead to sleep. If you want to sleep soundly, your sleeping environment should be as close to pitch black as possible and a little cooler than the average temperature of your home during the day—somewhere between 65 and 68 degrees Fahrenheit (18 and 20 degrees Celsius). A quick scan of Twitter can give you tons of inspiration on how to maintain a dark room even under challenging conditions. This post on using a hanger to seal wonky curtains in a hotel room, for example, is a great life hack:

Rick Klau ✔
@rklau

I don't remember who posted this on Twitter a few years ago, but whoever you are: you have improved every night I've spent in a hotel since.

11:43 PM · Oct 3, 2019 · Twitter for Android

- **Be consistent:** Sticking with a consistent sleep and wake time trains our bodies to fall asleep and wake up more efficiently. If you've ever taken a trip with a significant time change, you have seen the flipside of consistency. Moving your sleep and wake times creates a ton of turmoil for your body and brain. Whether you're flying from New York to Los Angeles or just going to bed three hours later on the weekend, to your body it's the same thing. Work back from when you need to wake up and try to consistently get to bed seven and a half hours beforehand. If you have an iPhone, the built-in Bedtime app can really help.

- **Work on your transition game:** Falling to sleep is a process that begins when you are awake. Jumping straight from processing stressful emails in front of a rectangle of blue light that slows your body's production of melatonin to climbing into bed and expecting to fall asleep immediately is like slamming on the brakes two feet before an intersection when you're doing 100 miles per hour and expecting to stop in time. You'll end up going through the whole process of working your way toward sleep while lying in bed wondering why you can't quiet your restless mind. When we are teaching newborn babies how to sleep, one of the most consistent pieces of parenting advice is to establish a sleep routine—something their brains begin to recognize as the signal to begin preparing for sleep—and it works for adults too. Physiologist and human performance expert Dr. Greg Wells recommends "defending the last hour" by putting away all electronic devices and reading a physical book, preferably fiction. For Phil Wilkins, his bedtime routine included the mindfulness app Headspace and James Patterson novels. Figure out what works for you and start to use it consistently.

GETTING SLEEP AHEAD OF PEAK PRESSURE MOMENTS

We have all been there: you have a big day coming up—a presentation, a test, a competition—and as a result you've made the effort to get to bed early. The room is dark, the alarm is set . . . and you're staring at the ceiling, wide awake, thinking about what's to come. As the minutes tick by, you watch your responsible sleep plan start to evaporate. You check the clock: it's 1 a.m. You realize that you're now heading toward a really important day on little sleep. Now the pressure of the upcoming event starts to get magnified by worry about lack of sleep. Your body's production of cortisol ramps up, your heart rate increases, and you're more awake than ever.

While the structure and routines you set up for the long haul will influence how easily you fall asleep ahead of your peak pressure moments, sometimes they're just not enough. As I've worked with high performers, I've learned a few specific hacks that can supplement good long-term sleep habits to help you fall asleep when you've got a big day ahead.

AN ELASTIC MINDSET

When I first started to establish a partnership between my firm, Third Factor, and the University of North Carolina's executive development group, it was a big deal for us. While we had always done work in the United States, it was our first major partnership, and it represented a significant opportunity to reach a new market with our services. Our first joint project was a large piece of work for a major financial institution based in Manhattan that was looking to embed a coaching culture in their wealth management organization. The project would entail workshops and coaching for over 800 managers across the United States, and—if we sold it—would be our biggest engagement of the year. The stakes were high: not only was the project itself important, but it would also serve as a litmus test in our relationship with UNC.

In December, the time had come to fly to New York and meet directly with the key stakeholders who would give the "go" or "no go" decision. I booked myself on a 6:00 p.m. flight the night before—lots of time to get in, get settled, and get a good night's rest before a big day. Three hours before my flight, I was on a conference call when I got a text message from the airline. The flight had been canceled due to inclement weather in New York, and I was rebooked onto a flight the next day that would see me miss the meeting. After an immediate surge of adrenaline and cortisol, I quickly excused myself from my call and started looking for options. Luckily there was an 8:30 p.m. flight on another airline that still had seats available, and I was able to secure a ticket.

When I arrived at the airport, it was clear that things were not going to go as planned. The departure boards were awash in red (flights that had been canceled) and yellow (flights that were delayed). As I sat at the gate, I watched the time for my flight slip steadily backward—to 9:30, to 10:55, to 11:45, to 12:50 a.m.— until, finally:

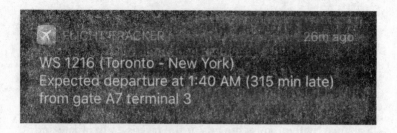

> **FLIGHT TRACKER**   26m ago
>
> WS 1216 (Toronto - New York)
> Expected departure at 1:40 AM (315 min late)
> from gate A7 terminal 3

In the end, my 8:30 p.m. flight departed at 1:49 a.m. and landed at LaGuardia at 3:16 a.m. I grabbed an Uber and made my way to Manhattan (with very light traffic, I might add), finally arriving at my hotel shortly after 4 a.m.

As I lay in bed, with my alarm set for 7:30, my mind started to race: "This meeting is so important, and I'm going in on three hours of sleep—this is a disaster." Worried that my already limited sleep would be further compressed by anxiety, I did what I've learned to do through frequent experience over the years: I reminded myself that, yes, sleep is important, but in the end one bad night of sleep won't derail my performance. I called to mind the multiple occasions I had flown overseas to present and done a good job after a couple of hours of poor-quality sleep in a red-eye plane seat, the presentations I had delivered when a bad cold had kept me up coughing late at night. All of these were data points that let me say, with confidence, not bravado, "You'll be fine." And as soon as I arrived at that place of acceptance and calm, I fell asleep.

An ability to put all of the plans in place for great sleep but then accept if it doesn't happen is another example of the dynamic tension between exerting control and accepting uncertainty that we explored earlier. Martha McCabe, the Olympic swimmer, really hammered this home when she talked about her approach to sleep at the Olympics. "Literally every single moment is planned," McCabe says. She planned in advance when she would wake up on race day, what she would eat, the time she would leave her hotel, the precise order of her prep at the pool, and when she would nap. At the same time, she realized that being overly attached to routine can cause its own stress. So she stayed flexible. "As rigid as [the routine] is," she says, "it's also very relaxed because there is a chance that you miss the bus or the race is early or late and so it's kind of keeping that rigid schedule but approaching it as one tiny step at a time and shifting it as need be." She found flexibility particularly important when it came to sleep. A nap was part of her routine, but if she didn't get one, she didn't let it affect her concentration. This attitude worked so well for her that, unbelievably, she was able to nap *between* her two races on race day at her first Olympic Games in London.

The next time you're lying awake ahead of a big day, remind yourself that sleep is important, but one night of lost sleep won't stop you from performing your best—knowing you'll be fine regardless may just allow you to drift off.

THE 100 CHALLENGE

As my wife would confirm, most of my good ideas aren't actually my ideas. They come from talking to others who have wrestled with their own issues and discovered solutions that work for them. The 100 challenge is a good example. It was shared with me by a colleague of Phil Wilkins as we talked through the issues around sleep that his story triggered.

While I can't take credit for the idea, I've made a couple of subtle tweaks as I've tinkered with it, and I can absolutely confirm that it works. The 100 challenge is the technique I turn to most consistently when I need to fall asleep and can't seem to convince my mind to let it happen. It's dead simple:

1. Start by holding a vivid image in your mind's eye of a room with a chalkboard or whiteboard at the front— it could be a school classroom, a meeting room at work, or something similar. For some reason, a chalkboard works best for me.

2. Imagine writing the number 100 in chalk or marker on the board. Hold the image of the numbers on the board steady for a second.

3. Imagine erasing the number, trying to really feel the process.

4. Imagine writing the number 99 where the 100 was, then erasing it.

5. Continue the process to 98, 97, 96, etcetera, and see how far down you can get.

The farthest I've ever made it in this exercise is the low 60s (the actual number is a bit hazy, since you really start to drift as you get closer to sleep). The person who taught it to me had once made it to 55.

You may be somewhat underwhelmed to discover that my high-performance secret for falling asleep is a variation on counting sheep, but there are ingenious tactics embedded in this technique that make it a good tool not just for falling asleep but also for honing a skill that is vital to performance under pressure.

First, this approach takes advantage of the fact that our brains are single-threaded processors: they can pay full attention to only one thing at a time. If you're working to vividly imagine the scenario—not just thinking of a number, but a number drawn in chalk on a physical blackboard, the feeling of the eraser wiping the number off, and so on—your brain is incapable of simultaneously focusing on the thoughts or feelings that are keeping you awake. Now, does this mean those thoughts won't occasionally break through? Of course not. You will be constantly distracted from your task, with the numbers disappearing and being replaced by unhelpful thoughts of the big day to come. But here's the beautiful thing: every time you consciously return your attention to the numbers on the chalkboard, you are practicing mindfulness, another vital skill that underpins performance under pressure. Framing each redirection as a mental rep in the gym—something that is strengthening your capacity for attentional control—is a great way to avoid getting frustrated.

Finally, framing this technique as a challenge—"Let's see how far I can get"—robs the passage of time of a sense of anxiety. Initially, you'll power through the numbers. But as you get farther down, you'll find your attention wandering more and more until it becomes a significant challenge to keep progressing. Eventually, your imagination will slip beyond your control and into the realm of dreams. Mission accomplished.

I'd love to hear how far you get. Let's see if you can beat the record.

THE BREATHING DRILL

As you've seen throughout this book, focusing on breathing is the most direct way to dramatically reduce energy levels in the body quickly when you're under pressure, which makes it a natural ally for falling asleep. Trying to focus on breathing when your mind is racing can be a Herculean task, however. As with the 100 challenge, it can be helpful to bring in a technique that can break the thought loops and aid in shifting your attention to breathing. A few years back I was taught a simple approach to breathing that forces concentration:

> AS YOU BREATHE IN, THINK THE WORD "OUT."
> AS YOU BREATHE OUT, THINK THE WORD "IN."

That's it. Go ahead—try it. You'll quickly find that it's almost impossible to do this effectively without some level of concentration. It's a great hack to quickly move your attention to your breathing by giving you a focal point for concentration.

Once you've gone through a few cycles of using the mental cue to keep your attention on your breathing, you can move to the "breathe low and breathe slow" technique introduced in Chapter 6. Bring your breathing down to 6 breaths per minute and focus on filling your diaphragm.

Finally, add in a timing element: work to try to make your exhalation roughly twice as long as your inhalation. We've known since Dr. Herbert Benson's landmark book *The Relaxation Response* in 1975 that a shorter inhalation and longer exhalation triggers the body's natural relaxation processes, and subsequent research has identified that a 1:2 breathing pattern tells the vagus nerve to deliver a message to the brain that triggers the parasympathetic nervous system. Try inhaling to the count of four and exhaling to the count of eight, which will keep you on a roughly 10-seconds-per-breath count.

See how long you can focus on your breathing, keeping it low, slow, and in a 1:2 ratio. When your brain inevitably wanders, keep doing your mental reps to bring yourself back to center as your body and brain relax.

EATING FOR ENERGY

The number of things the human body accomplishes simply by breaking down food is truly miraculous. When my wife was pregnant with our first child, I found that one of the most surefire ways to irritate her was to talk about how she was literally building our baby out of food. "Stop taking this miraculous process and turning it into something so gross," she would say. But to me, pregnancy is the ultimate expression of the (female) body's ingenuity. How is it possible that by inserting nothing other than food and water—mostly orange Popsicles in the case of our oldest, Jack—the body can construct eyeballs, a heart, a brain, a liver, bones, skin, cartilage, and fingernails? Oh, and by the way, at the same time it's also converting that food into heat, kinetic energy, blood, bile, and everything else that keeps the world's most complex organism functioning. When you consider that food and water are the only inputs to a closed system that produces such a remarkable variety of outputs, it really is something.

The fact that food and water are our only inputs means that, unsurprisingly, they are absolutely vital to our health and functioning over the long haul. The degree to which we can approach the volume of a busy life without feeling exhausted at the end of the day, week, or month is directly correlated to what and how we eat.

Nicole Springle is a registered dietitian and the lead for sport nutrition at the Canadian Sport Institute Ontario. CSIO is a remarkable facility, located in Toronto, that is accessible only to Olympic and Paralympic athletes and teams. An interdisciplinary team housed in a cutting-edge facility ensures that these athletes are applying the best in sport science and medicine to optimize their performance. A big part of that performance is, of course, nutrition. In her role as lead for sport nutrition, Springle works individually with athletes to craft tailored nutrition plans for training, competition, and recovery, and also holds classes in CSIO's teaching kitchen to help athletes learn how to prepare snacks and meals to support their performance.

For Springle, there is one big mental shift that underpins all of the advice she provides to elite athletes: "Most people eat to survive—eating is something that they do to satiate hunger," she says, "but the people who really perform over the long haul are those who shift to thinking about food as fuel for performance, as a source of energy." According to Springle, the energy peaks and troughs most of us encounter throughout the day are heavily influenced by the impact on our blood sugar levels of what and when we eat. Refined sugar gets a deservedly bad rap, but the natural sugar that is a by-product of breaking down wholesome food is the preferred fuel for our muscles, brain, and other organs and is the basic energy source that underpins our body's function.

At the risk of oversimplifying a fairly complex process, our blood sugar levels throughout the day are predominantly a result of two things: eating pushes the levels up, and, in response, our body produces insulin to bring them back down, resulting in an up-and-down rhythm throughout the day. In order to have consistent, optimal energy and focus, our goal is to keep the ups and downs within a consistent, moderate range. When blood sugar gets too high or too low, we become lethargic and our concentration starts to falter. Of course, as anyone who has dealt with or supported someone with diabetes knows, when blood sugar gets to clinically low levels, it can have severe and potentially fatal consequences.

When Springle starts working with an athlete, the first thing she does is learn their current eating patterns to map out the rhythm of their blood sugar for the day. One elite golfer she worked with shared the following routine:

- 7 a.m. wake up and a breakfast of banana, yogurt, and coffee.
- A balanced, healthy lunch at 11 a.m.
- A granola bar at 3 p.m.—"usually the kind dipped in chocolate," he admitted.
- Practice from 3–7 p.m.
- A big dinner at 8 p.m.
- Despite his best efforts, usually some kind of a sweets binge before bed at 10 p.m.

When Springle mapped this pattern into a view of his blood sugar levels, it was clear that there were some issues:

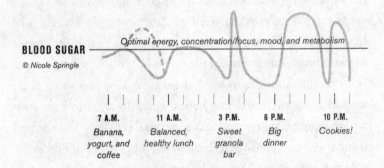

First, the small breakfast he was eating wasn't enough to carry him through to lunch—his blood sugar started to dip almost immediately after the meal. The effect of low blood sugar was masked, however, by the caffeine in his coffee, shown by the dotted line. This meant that he suffered an energy crash and an immediate and pressing feeling of hunger when the effect of the caffeine wore off around 10:30, and he showed up to lunch hungry and early.

Second, the sweet granola bar at 3 p.m. produced a spike in blood sugar that sent his body into insulin overdrive to quickly get his levels down, which led to an energy crash just when he needed energy the most for his 3–7 p.m. practice. Coming out of practice, he was starving and tucked into a big dinner. As Springle notes, "People sometimes think that sweet foods are the only things that push blood sugar up, but a big dinner does the same thing." She calls what happens next the "turkey dinner effect." We eat a massive meal (think Christmas or Thanksgiving), and we head to the couch feeling overstuffed—like we can't possibly eat anything more. "And then, 30 minutes later, the desserts come out," Springle says, "and we start to crave something sweet." This is a by-product of the insulin surging into our body to counteract the rise in blood sugar. As the insulin takes sugar out of our bloodstream, even though we're satiated, our body starts to crave sugar, and we tuck into the pumpkin pie.

Eating for resilience under pressure isn't about counting calories, going paleo, cutting out meat, or fasting. While there are lots of reasons that one of those approaches might make sense for your unique circumstances or goals (weight loss, food sensitivity, disease management, and so on), when it comes to the basics of handling a high-volume life over the long haul, the most effective strategy is to see food as a source of performance fuel and eat in ways that smooth out the ups and downs during the day so that you stabilize mood and concentration. The easiest way to do that is to remember three basic principles: avoid crashes by eating every three to four hours, smooth out rises and falls by combining carbohydrates and protein, and eliminate spikes by choosing carbohydrates with a low glycemic index (GI).

AVOID CRASHES BY EATING EVERY THREE TO FOUR HOURS

Hunger and low blood sugar are a bad combination when it comes to navigating pressure. A wide body of research shows that people in a glucose-depleted state "tend to be more impulsive, punitive, and aggressive"—none of which are ideal for navigating high-stakes situations. In addition, studies demonstrate (and most of us have personally experienced) a link between hunger and negative mood. There is a reason we have terms like "food mood" and "hangry." To avoid the crashes, Springle recommends avoiding going longer than four hours without eating a meal or a snack. When you do eat, despite what the commercials tell you, don't just grab a Snickers bar; instead, follow the advice in the two principles that follow. *What* you eat every three to four hours is just as important as when you eat.

SMOOTH OUT RISES AND FALLS BY COMBINING CARBS AND PROTEIN

When Springle designed a program for the elite golfer she was coaching, she ended up with the approach illustrated in the following diagram:

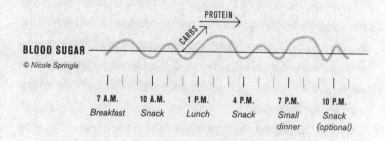

© Nicole Springle

First, you'll note that it takes advantage of the previous principle and spaces eating out every three to four hours. Equally important, however, is ensuring that each meal or snack both gives the athlete an immediate boost *and* delivers long-lasting, smooth energy. The secret to this two-pronged approach is to balance carbohydrates and protein with every snack or meal.

As Springle notes, carbs are rapidly absorbed by the body, giving you a blood sugar boost that will quickly provide energy, improve mood, and sharpen concentration, but it's protein that will make the benefits last until the next snack or meal, three to four hours later. Designing meals and snacks that balance carbs and protein is a vital part of eating for performance. You can find a hugely helpful and practical list of snacks that meet Springle's exacting requirements for athletes on page 209.

ELIMINATE SPIKES BY CHOOSING LOW-GI CARBS

Given the plethora of attention given to Atkins, keto, and paleo diets, all of which are low-carb, you may be surprised to see a recommendation to eat carbohydrates with every meal and snack.

In many quarters, carbs are about as popular as taxes and paper cuts. And it is widely agreed that the old food guide recommendations to make grains and other carbohydrates the base of the food pyramid was not good advice—we should be eating far more protein than we were advised in the past and fewer carbs. In short, carbs are complicated.

One of the biggest red flags in the elite golfer's routine was the dose of carbs in the form of a sugary granola bar at 3 p.m. That led to a huge spike and then sudden crash in blood sugar. This is the downside of some carbs: they flood the body with sugar, which triggers a massive insulin response and a quick crash. And yet, when it comes to achieving smooth and even blood sugar levels, there is a vital role for carbohydrates. The key is choosing carbs that are low on the glycemic index, which measures how quickly the body converts carbs into sugar. Pure glucose has a GI of 100, and, according to research from the National Institutes of Health focused on people with type 2 diabetes, "carbohydrates with a low GI value (55 or less) are more slowly digested, absorbed, and metabolized and cause a lower and slower rise in blood glucose and, therefore, insulin levels." So, when it comes to carbs, think rolled oats (GI of 55) and carrots (GI of 39) instead of corn flakes (GI of 81) and boiled potatoes (GI of 78).

You'll find a list of the GIs of thousands of foods at www .glycemicindex.com, a site maintained by the University of Sydney's Glycemic Index Research Service.

BALANCED SNACKING IDEAS
FROM NICOLE SPRINGLE

SNACK FROM HOME OR ON THE ROAD

- ⅓–¾ cup yogurt and a piece of fruit
- 1–2 oz cheese and 4–6 whole-wheat crackers or 1–3 lavash crackers
- ½–¾ cup low-fat cottage cheese and ½ cup blueberries, chopped pineapple, etc.
- 1–2 tbsp peanut or almond butter with apple, banana, celery, etc.
- 1–2 cups plain milk, chocolate milk, or soy beverage
- 1 mini can flavored tuna or salmon and 4–6 whole-grain crackers
- 10–23 almonds and 1 piece of fruit (apple, pear, 1 cup grapes, etc.)
- ¼ cup hummus and ½ cup fresh veggies or ½ whole-wheat pita
- ⅓–1 cup whole-grain cereal and ½–1 cup milk
- 1 hard-boiled egg and a slice of whole-wheat toast or ½ cup chopped veggies
- 1–2 tbsp peanut or almond butter on a whole-wheat English muffin
- Banana and milk or soy beverage shake (see **Rapid Snack #1**)
- 1–2 cheese strings or Mini Babybel cheese with crackers, fruit, or veggies
- ½ cup plain yogurt, ¼ cup Bran Buds or low-fat granola, and berries
- ½ cup unsweetened applesauce and ½ cup plain yogurt
- Bean burrito (see **Rapid Snack #2**)
- 1 cup quinoa or couscous salad with chickpeas or other beans
- 2–4 slices lean deli meat or leftover meat on ½–1 whole-wheat wrap
- ½ cup edamame or chickpeas
- 1 cup cooked oatmeal, served with ¾ cup milk or soy beverage
- 1 cup bean-, lentil-, or meat-based soup (look for at least 5 g protein)
- Cottage cheese, raisins, and sunflower seeds (see **Rapid Snack #3**)
- Energy bar (look for 7–10 g protein and < 250 calories)
- 1 slice whole-wheat toast or English muffin with 1 oz light cheddar cheese and tomato
- ½ cup chopped veggies, dipped in ½ cup low-fat refried beans

SNACK FROM HOME OR ON THE ROAD

- 1 cup meat or vegetarian chili
- ½ cup bean salad, made with red and white kidney beans, chick-peas, and vinaigrette dressing (can buy premade)
- ¼ cup trail mix, made with dry-roasted soybeans (see **Rapid Snack #4**), and a piece of fruit
- ½ cup low-fat ricotta cheese and ½ cup raspberries or canned peaches
- ¼ pound silken tofu with banana and orange juice, mixed in blender

FAST FOOD, CAFETERIA, OR RESTAURANT CHOICES

- Meat or vegetarian chili
- Garden salad with grilled chicken, turkey, egg, chickpeas, cheese, etc.
- Container of cottage cheese, yogurt, milk or chocolate milk, and 1 fruit
- Meat- or bean-based soup
- 6-inch whole-wheat sub with lean meat, veggies, and mustard
- Tuna, chicken, or ham in whole-wheat pita or wrap

RAPID SNACK #1: FROZEN FRUIT SHAKE

- 1 frozen banana (peel and freeze in a resealable bag when it turns brown)
- ¾ cup milk or soy beverage
- Berries (fresh or frozen) to taste
- Splash of orange juice

Combine all ingredients in a blender and blend until smooth. Serve immediately.

RAPID SNACK #2: REFRIED BEAN BURRITO

- ½ cup (4–6 generous tbsp) low-fat refried beans
- 1 oz low-fat cheese
- 6- or 12-inch whole-wheat tortilla
- ½ tomato, diced
- Low-fat sour cream and salsa

Combine beans and cheese in a bowl and microwave for 1–2 minutes, until cheese is melted. Spread over half the tortilla and add tomato on top. Fold tortilla and cut into slices. Serve with sour cream and salsa.

RAPID SNACK #3: PM "HOLD ME OVER"

- ½ cup low-fat cottage cheese
- 2 tbsp raisins
- 2 tbsp sunflower seeds
- Ground cinnamon, to taste

Combine all ingredients in a small resealable container. Enjoy as needed to curb cravings and hunger, usually mid-afternoon, at work, school, practice, etc.

RAPID SNACK #4: TRAIL MIX

- 2 parts dry-roasted soybeans
- 2 parts cereal (such as Shreddies or Cheerios)
- 1 part raisins
- 1 part Bran Buds
- 1 part dry-roasted almonds or sunflower seeds

Combine all ingredients in a small resealable container. To reduce calories, use more cereal and fewer dried fruits and nuts. Dry-roasted soybeans are a lower-calorie alternative to other nuts. Serving size = ¼ cup (try to portion out individually if you are prone to overeating).

- For lasting fullness and energy, and to reduce cravings and overeating at home, combine protein and carbohydrate foods at meals and snacks. Each of the snacks listed contains both protein and carbs.
- When choosing meats, choose leaner options like chicken or turkey, lean roast beef, or ham. Avoid sausage, salami, bologna, or other more highly processed meats, which are much higher in total fat and saturated fat.
- For grains, look for 100% whole-grain or whole-wheat options rather than those containing "enriched wheat flour."

MOVEMENT IS MEDICINE

When it comes to building a solid foundation that will allow you to thrive under pressure, the third leg of the stool is movement. Of course, exercise provides numerous long-term benefits: a lower risk of cancer and type 2 diabetes, delayed onset of dementia and other neurodegenerative diseases, prevention of bone density loss, and many more. Consistent exercise is a wonderful way to improve both your lifespan and your "health span"—that is, the number of years you remain physically and mentally capable, not just alive and breathing.

All of those benefits are terrific over the fullness of a life, but when we're under a high-volume load, exercise is often the first thing we abandon. It can be hard to focus on delaying the potential onset of dementia in 30 years when we have a massive client presentation coming up in three weeks, the balance of work and family to navigate, or (purely hypothetically) a looming deadline to deliver a manuscript to your book publisher. And yet, when we are under the gun, exercise has a big role to play, emotionally, cognitively, and physically.

The life of a firefighter is one of extremes. A large portion of their time is spent doing, well, not a lot. And then the bell rings and they are thrust into a massively high-stakes, high-uncertainty environment. How they react when the bell rings—what happens to their blood pressure, heart rate, and other measures of physical response—can have a dramatic impact on their performance. To test the links between exercise and a firefighter's physical response to stress, researchers from the University of Texas at Austin recruited volunteers from the Austin Fire Department. First, the entire group had baseline measurements taken of blood pressure and heart rate at rest and in a "stress" scenario that was induced by a computerized version of the Austin Fire Department's strategy and tactics drill—a simulated fire response scenario. Then the group was split in two. One half, the fitness group, undertook a 16-week supervised exercise regimen that consisted of four 40-minute sessions per week on a rowing machine, while the other served as a control group and continued their usual physical routine. At the end of the period, the same measurements were taken again. Unsurprisingly, the fitness group showed improvements in their physical capacity. Here's the more interesting part: they also demonstrated a reduced physical response to stress. Although there were no differences between the groups before the 16-week program, after it the people on the rowing program showed a smaller increase in both blood pressure and heart rate during the stress scenario. In addition, "Rowers reported less stress-related anxiety and negative affect. Thus, not only did rowing provide increases in physical fitness, it also served to lessen reactivity to firefighting-related psychological stress." The results from this and similar studies provide compelling evidence of an inverse relationship between exercise and sensitivity to stress. The more we exercise, the less likely we are to be thrown into a hyper-activated state under pressure.

Beyond tempering activation, exercise also improves our emotional state under pressure. The findings in the firefighter study that showed a link between exercise and anxiety have been widely reproduced. A study of 55,000 adults in North America found that people who exercised had fewer symptoms of anxiety and depression, and a meta-analysis of 70 studies showed that exercise improves mood and lessens anxiety in adults who don't meet the clinical definition for depression. Especially over the long haul of a high-volume life, non-clinical anxiety can be a constant companion; exercise helps to keep it at bay.

So, how do you access all of these great benefits when you're under pressure? This is probably the best part of the exercise research, because the answer is simple: just move. A study out of the Harvard T.H. Chan School of Public Health on the links between exercise and depression showed that anyone who regularly "replaced 15 minutes of sitting with 15 minutes of running, or one hour of sitting with one hour of moderate activity like brisk walking" experienced the mood-stabilizing benefits of exercise. There are certainly health benefits to engaging in more strenuous exercise, such as high-intensity interval training or strength training, and in general the more intense the exercise you undertake the shorter the amount of time required for you to reap the benefits, but when it comes to performing under pressure, there is no requirement that you buy kettlebells or sign up for a CrossFit membership. Just move.

JUMPSTARTING THE VIRTUOUS CYCLE AND STAYING FLEXIBLE

I've presented each of these areas as if they are independent of each other, but of course they aren't. In his terrific book *The Ripple Effect*, physiologist and human performance expert Dr. Greg Wells does a terrific job of showing how sleep, nutrition, movement, and performance are all interconnected. If we sleep better, we'll eat better. If we move more, we'll sleep better. If we eat better, we'll think better. If we think better, we'll sleep more. Once you start positive momentum in one area, it ripples into other areas of your life. Starting a positive feedback loop simply requires getting started.

On the other hand, falling off the wagon in one area isn't the end of the world. There are times in our lives when it's just not feasible to get eight hours of sleep a night, maintain our workouts, and eat carefully calibrated meals and snacks every three to four hours. Yes, with careful planning we can develop better routines and habits, but sometimes, when we're under pressure, even the best of intentions get sidelined for a period of time. In the process of writing this book, for example, I adopted a routine of getting up early and writing from 6 to 8 a.m. while my wife got our three kids ready for school. The trade-off was that she needed me to watch the kids while she got in her workouts after I finished working at the end of the day. By the time the kids were in bed and we'd cleaned up from dinner, there wasn't a lot of time left for me to exercise, especially if I wanted any time with my wife. So, for a three-month period while I was writing the bulk of the book, I made the decision to focus on sleep and nutrition and forgive myself for missing workouts. When the book was done, I turned my attention back to getting all of my workouts in. Now, if I had started to notice my mood or the quality of my sleep degrading, I would have reevaluated that routine. But it ended up working for me.

This is what I called an elastic mindset earlier: an ability to let certain things go when necessary, to avoid adding another layer of pressure from your own expectations and guilt on top of an already busy and productive life. In the end, we are all just doing the best we can, so pick the habits that will give you the fuel you need but forgive yourself if your self-care is imperfect.

PART 3
PUTTING IT ALL TOGETHER

CHAPTER 10

THE LIMITS OF INDEPENDENCE

RECRUITING SUPPORT THAT WORKS

In early 2010, my father noticed a bulge on his neck. It was small at first, but it continued to grow. At the time, he was busy preparing for the Vancouver Olympics and had other things to worry about—notably, his work with the Canadian Women's Hockey Team (who would end up winning gold). When he got to Vancouver, however, the team physician took one look at it and advised him to get a biopsy immediately on returning home. And so, after the excitement and triumph of the Games, he headed to the doctor for a checkup. When the results came back, it was what we had feared—and it was a little more complicated. The mass in his neck wasn't itself cancerous, but it contained marker cells that are only produced by malignant tumors. There was a tumor somewhere in his throat. He had squamous cell throat cancer.

There was a catch, however: they couldn't locate the primary tumor. The team at the Princess Margaret Cancer Centre could see the cast-off cells in the neck bulge, but couldn't find the source with any of the many MRIs and biopsies they performed. This ruled out a targeted course of radiation therapy that would focus specifically on the tumor sites. They would need to radiate his entire neck, a scorched-earth approach that meant his salivary glands would never produce saliva again and he would receive a much higher dose of radiation than a typical patient. All in all, it would require 35 radiation treatments—five days a week for seven weeks—and three doses of chemo at one, four, and seven weeks.

As a result of a life full of optimism, generosity, and general helpfulness, my father has an exceptional group of close friends, and in the face of this daunting regimen, they banded together to create a formidable support network. Working with my mom, they mapped out a schedule of who would drive him down to each treatment, stay there for the duration, and then drive him home.

When my dad became aware of the schedule, his reaction wasn't exactly what they had anticipated: "I'll be driving myself to these treatments," he informed my mom. My father, like many who seek out challenging, high-pressure lives, is fiercely independent. And yet, as he discovered through the harrowing few months that followed his bold proclamation, independence can be detrimental under pressure when it manifests as an inability to seek or accept support. After a couple of weeks of treatment, the insertion of a feeding tube, a tough course of chemo, and the general exhaustion of what his body was going through, he relented and accepted that he did need help. As he said: "I realized that while in the end I needed to do it myself, I didn't need to do it alone."

Seeking support is a vital skill when it comes to managing pressure, both in the moment and over the long haul. When we rely too heavily on our independence, we fail to tap into a vital resource to help us buffer stress, and we rob ourselves of an opportunity to feel a sense of connection and common purpose. However, your support network must be carefully constructed; otherwise, there's a risk that, rather than easing your pressure, it may actually contribute *more* pressure. This is one of the most surprising things I've learned in the interviews I've conducted. There's no question that support can be helpful during times of pressure, but the wrong type can also create problems. Sometimes, people acting with the best intentions unwittingly cause more stress for the person they're trying to help.

Learning how to build a support network that really works for you will ease your burden when you're under pressure, and understanding the subtleties of what is helpful and what isn't will also enable you to offer better support to others.

WHEN SUPPORT GOES SIDEWAYS

At the outset of my research, I held a belief that the more support you recruited when under pressure the better, and that a key pressure trap was an inability or unwillingness to reach out for support lest you appear weak or incompetent. The reality is much more nuanced. There is no question that support is vital; in my father's ultimately successful battle with cancer, support eventually became the single biggest factor allowing him to navigate a period of great pressure. And yet not all support is helpful. How you gather support matters: how many people you involve, the experience and personality those people bring to the table, how effectively you direct your support network toward behaviors that are helpful and away from those that are unhelpful— all of these influence whether the support will work for you or against you.

In general, a poorly constructed support network reveals itself in one of three ways: it turns into a pity party, other people's emotions get added to your pile, or the stakes are raised on something that you already know is important.

THE PITY PARTY

Here's the most pressure Heidi Tourond has ever been under: "It was the day my husband walked out. We had two kids and he said, 'I'm leaving and you're on your own.' I was unemployed, had been out of the workforce for 16 years, and I had to figure out what to do to pay the bills and survive."

Tourond had been married for all of those 16 "unemployed" years, busy working in the home and raising two boys who were now 14 and 15. "They were two boys highly involved in sports, in school, and all kinds of activities. I had always been there—I'd been home since the day they were born and before that. So, suddenly, it's a critical time in their life and their home's been disrupted. And they didn't see it coming at all. So you're trying to deal with the fallout that they might have and, again, keep yourself together."

Tourond faced not only a chaotic disruption for her boys, but a battle for survival. When her husband left, she had just a few weeks' worth of savings. With no recent work experience, she had less than two months to find a job or default on her mortgage, car payments, and everything else that doesn't go away just because you've experienced a traumatic event. Faced with the enormity of the challenge, and processing tremendous personal grief and betrayal, Tourond did a profoundly human thing: "I literally laid on the bathroom floor for two days and cried." As she lay crying, two voices were warring in her head: an inner critic, the internalized voice of her ex-husband, who was saying, "You can't do this—this is too much for you," and a second voice saying, "I'm going to prove you wrong."

Eventually she decided it was time for a change of pace—and scenery. "After two days of crying, I went, 'Okay, that wasn't helpful. Let's figure out how we're going to get through this.'" Picking herself up off the floor, she started to plan for action. She broke down the overwhelming task ahead of her into small steps that she could make progress on: put together a résumé, buy clothes for job interviews. "I made a step-by-step plan. It took me maybe three weeks to figure it all out." This pivot from fear to planning—made possible by identifying where she could exert control, breaking the task down into small steps, and starting to make progress—is what Tourond, now a successful executive, points to as the pivotal moment in her eventual triumph over adversity.

Not everyone was ready to make the pivot with her, though. "There was no time for the pity party, but people seemed to want to throw one for me," says Tourond. Despite her inner resolve to move forward, many people around her were fixated on commiseration. "I think people thought that they were being supportive, that we could all sit there and go, 'Woe is me,' and I didn't want that. That wasn't helpful. That was just wallowing in it. And after two days, I had already decided that I wasn't going to do that."

Paradoxically, it was people outside her support network who were more helpful—specifically, the people and resources who could help her execute her plan. "It was really, Okay, what is the path of least resistance? And the path was that if I don't know how to do something, I need to go to somebody that does." She contacted an employment agency, which helped her put her résumé together and set up job interviews. With their support, she nailed the very first interview and got her first paying job in 16 years. Four months later, she got a promotion and a raise. Five years later, she was making more money than her husband ever had.

Tourond's support network wanted to keep the focus on the past and unintentionally added fuel to the voice of her inner critic—the one feeling overwhelmed and outmatched. Tourond ultimately summed up her as experience as "No one else is going to fix me but me." And she did.

When our support system is merely one that sits and talks about how bad everything is, we are having what Benjamin Zander, the remarkable conductor of the Boston Philharmonic Orchestra, has called "the conversation of no possibilities." It can make us feel close to other people, but it ultimately doesn't get us anywhere.

THE EMOTIONAL CASCADERS
Anne Merklinger is the CEO of Own the Podium (OTP), an organization with one focus: maximizing Canada's medal production at the Olympic and Paralympic Games. OTP is entirely in

the support role when it comes to sport. They provide technical guidance to organizations like Swimming Canada or Wheelchair Basketball Canada that have athletes or teams with medal potential in the next eight years, and they help direct over $85 million in funding from the Canadian government, the Canadian Olympic Committee, and the Canadian Paralympic Committee to the places where it can have the greatest impact on medals. As Merklinger says, she and her team "are not on the starting blocks or at the start line. We're not performing. We are trying to provide sport organizations with all of the competencies, skills, resources, best practices, guidance, and suggestions to help their athletes perform on demand."

For every Games, OTP publishes an overview of how many medals Canada might win. "Six months out from the Games, we will say, 'Based on our technical analysis, we have medal potential in x number of sports.'" The projection gets broken down further into "strong," "moderate," and "low" potential, and a certain number of medals becomes the benchmark for Games success. In Canada, this prediction is highly visible—OTP's prognosis is published in all of the major national newspapers, typically accompanied by commentary from Merklinger. And because Merklinger is the face of the projection, and a visible steward of $80 million in tax dollars, she is held publicly accountable for performance after the fact.

For all the levers Merklinger and OTP can pull in the eight years leading up to each of the Games, at the end of the day it's up to the athletes to perform. As Merklinger says, "We don't just mail the medals to the people who are top-ranked." Nothing that has happened before the Games matters; the athletes and teams need to peak at exactly the right moment. During the Games,

Merklinger is in a unique position: she has none of the pressure to perform but feels all the stress of the outcome.

Merklinger is also uniquely qualified to evaluate the stress of a support role relative to the pressure of a performance role. Earlier in life, she was an elite curler: "I was a skip, I threw last. We got points on the scoreboard if I made my shot and we didn't if I missed my shot." Despite this pressure, Merklinger was able to focus on the process instead of the outcome: "Hit the broom, throw the right weight—all those kinds of mechanical or procedural thoughts. I never thought, *Gosh, if I miss this shot, then this will happen.*"

She contrasts that with her experience as the head of OTP at the 2016 Rio Games. OTP had predicted that Canada would win 19 or more medals. With two days left in the Games, they had won 17, and Merklinger was nervous as she looked ahead. She couldn't see a clear path to the goal. "I knew the consequence. We felt a tremendous amount of pressure around that. This was our entire organization's responsibility, and if we didn't achieve that objective, there would be consequences for the organization, our team, and all of the people that had worked so hard to help Canada achieve that objective. That responsibility for me as the CEO was overwhelming." Then, on the eve of the final day, race walker Evan Dunfee was awarded a bronze medal after the racer ahead of him was disqualified, raising the total to 18. The target was in sight, but there was no margin for error. It all came down to the women's soccer team, who were playing in a bronze medal match on the final day of the Games against the home team, Brazil.

Merklinger was in Rio de Janeiro, and the game was in São Paolo, which left her watching it on TV with other Canadians, perched on the edge of her seat. Canada played a strong first half and led 1–0 heading into halftime. Then, 52 minutes into the game, captain Christine Sinclair scored her third goal of the tournament—a goal that would end up sealing a 2–1 win over a talented Brazilian team and their 70,000 screaming fans. The victory delivered Canada's first-ever medal in soccer and bumped Team Canada up to 19 medals. "I was emotionally overcome by it," says Merklinger. For her, it was much more stressful to be in a support role than to be a performer.

While not all of us feel the weight of an entire nation's performance at the Olympics, everyone who supports others knows how it feels to be invested in an outcome that is in someone else's hands. When our child takes the field or the stage, when a close colleague pitches to a big client, when a friend texts us as they wait for a high-stakes exam or job interview, their emotions are contagious. We experience their anxiety, fear, and worry—all the emotions associated with pressure—without being able to take direct action to mitigate the pressure or affect the outcome. This is the crucial delineation between stress and pressure I outlined in Chapter 1. Before the Rio Games, Merklinger talked extensively with her team about how to handle the emotion: "Every single day we would go for a 40- to 50-minute run and talk about the things we could influence: our messaging to the public and media, debriefing going forward, etcetera." Their goal was to not let their emotion interfere with their support role.

Unfortunately, not everyone in a support role is as savvy as Merklinger. When we're recruiting a support network, we need to be aware that our supporters' inability to take direct action can create a situation where the very people we are turning to are unwittingly caught in their own helplessness loop, and their only clear path to direct action is through us.

In Chapter 6, we met Sean St. John, a banker who was diagnosed with testicular cancer in his mid-20s. One of the more fascinating aspects of his story was how he approached support: "I would say that maybe two or three people in the office might've known [that I was battling cancer] . . . and on the family side of things I remember not talking to anybody that much at all." For St. John, keeping his diagnosis to himself was a mechanism for minimizing pressure: "I didn't want people to worry about it—it was easier for me to take it on myself and not have the stress of trying to make sure everybody else was okay."

This is a theme I heard repeatedly in interviews. The emotions of the people in support roles end up becoming an additional source of pressure, adding their weight to the pressure of performance we are already navigating.

THE STAKE-RAISERS

One of the secrets of high performance is to surround yourself with people who see that you are capable of more than you think. As speaker Jim Rohn memorably said: "You are the average of the five people you spend the most time with." Over the long haul, you want to be around people who set expectations high and push you to reach your potential. These allies hold you true to who you are, remind you when you are behaving in ways that aren't aligned with your values, and encourage you to dig deeper, work harder, and aim higher. What these strong supporters share is that they are focused on elevating the *inputs*—namely your mindset and behavior. Too often we end up with support networks that, under the guise of being helpful, focus on elevating the importance of the *outputs*.

When Heidi Tourond's husband walked out, in addition to navigating a group of friends determined to throw her a pity party, she had a conversation ringing in her ears from 15 years earlier: "My first son had just been born. I remember calling my mother, crying and saying, 'Mom, I have to leave. I can't stay with this man; he's cruel to me.' And she said, 'You are a wife and you are a mother and you have an obligation to stay or you let your child down.'"

This type of support has only one impact: raising the stakes on something that we already know matters. Tourond was acutely aware of the potential impact of a divorce on her kids. Redirecting focus back to the outcome counteracts the vital skill of determining what's *not* at stake that we learned in Chapter 5 and compromises our ability to see the challenges in our lives in the proper perspective. Her mother's version of support ultimately led to a magnification of the peak pressure moments that were to come years later for Tourond. When her husband left, she felt both the pressure to survive and a sense of failure.

TAPPING INTO THE VALUE OF SOCIAL SUPPORT

Reading through all the ways support can go wrong, you might begin to wonder if it has any value at all. And you may be worried that, in your attempts to provide support to others, you've been unwittingly creating additional stress for them through a bunch of entirely understandable and well-meaning endeavors like trying to empathize (the pity party), not being perfectly stoic (adding the weight of your emotions), or getting excited about the outcome (raising the stakes).

The reality is that there are few things in life that are more correlated to resilience and health outcomes than social support. One study of Vietnam combat veterans who were receiving treatment for post-traumatic stress disorder (PTSD) showed that it was the level of homecoming stress—in particular the degree of support they received during their first six months after returning from the theater of war—that most directly influenced their PTSD. The authors wrote: "homecoming stress was the most significant predictor of current PTSD symptomatology superseding combat exposure, childhood and civilian traumas, and stressful life events."

Beyond the acute stress that accompanies combat, a general analysis of the literature on the relationship between social support and resilience undertaken by the National Institutes of Health concluded that "the effect of social support on life expectancy appears to be as strong as the effects of obesity, cigarette smoking, hypertension, or level of activity" and that "the relationship between good social support and superior mental and physical health has been observed in diverse populations, including college students, unemployed workers, new mothers, widows, and parents of children with serious mental illnesses."

One of the most famous studies in all of the social sciences is a long-term one, run out of Harvard, known as the Grant Study. It began in the early 1940s, when the patron, Mr. Grant, provided research funding to answer the question "What is it that constitutes 'the good life'?" A pretty big research question indeed. To start answering it, the researchers recruited over 300 people from the

Harvard graduating classes of 1939 through 1944 and began to follow them through their lives. Eventually, they realized that a group of male Harvard undergraduates probably wasn't the most representative sample of the population, and so, roughly 25 years later, they added a second cohort that was slightly more diverse. On an annual basis, they would bring each participant into the lab and perform a battery of medical tests—things like blood pressure, body composition, and so on. The tests evolved over time as medicine became more sophisticated. And they also did qualitative research to understand what had transpired in the subjects' lives over the preceding year: major accomplishments, setbacks, triumphs, and tragedies.

The remarkable thing is that this study is still going on today. There are some participants left from that second cohort, all in their 90s now. And through the decades, researchers have built up an unprecedented view of the lives of 724 men—some well lived and others filled with regrets and missed opportunities.

A man named George Vaillant was the caretaker of the study for 30 years, until 2003. It became his life's work to follow the group and extract insights into research papers, books, and even a terrific TED talk. He also published an annual newsletter that went out to the remaining members of the study. In 2008, one of the members asked a simple question: "What is the one most important thing that you have learned from this study?" Vaillant's answer was succinct. He said, "I have learned that in the end the only thing that matters are your connections to other people." In surveying the accumulated data from hundreds of lives across almost seven decades, that was the number one predictor of whether people felt they had lived "a good life."

In short, supportive relationships matter—at all times, and especially when we are under pressure. Simply retreating or withdrawing because support *can* be an added source of pressure is a quick way to rob yourself of one of the most effective buffers against pressure.

So how do we tap into the immense value of social support while avoiding the potential pitfalls? There are three themes that I've heard repeatedly about creating support systems that work:

1. **Keep it tight:** When it comes to support networks, size matters.
2. **Recruit from "inside the arena":** Fellow combatants are more helpful than spectators.
3. **Set the terms of engagement proactively:** Tell your supporters exactly what you need from them; don't just "take what you can get."

KEEP IT TIGHT

The stress created by a support network is directly proportional to its size. We've seen how volume creates pressure, and that's just as true of support as it is of stressors. Too many cooks in the kitchen, no matter how helpful they are trying to be, create pressure for the chef. When pressure is imminent, close ranks.

In Olympic swimmer Martha McCabe's case, a key step in her Olympic preparation was to zero out her support network by cutting off access to everyone, and then selectively let people into her circle by giving out a new phone number. As the pressure intensified, she narrowed down to just a few key people: teammates, coaches, and support staff. This reduction in the size of her support network corresponded to greater use of it—she had more frequent contact and was more open with a smaller number of people.

Jenn Cruz, who got locked in a stairwell in the midst of one of the defining moments of her career, related a similar insight. The number one thing that helped her recover from the emotional aftermath of what she perceived as a significant failure was tapping into a small, close support network. "My close supports are my two sisters, my cousin, and another one of my best friends. What is that? Five of us? We have a WhatsApp thread that we're constantly on, so it's like an ongoing conversation, and it's very easy to tap into that. All of them, really, there's just no judgment. They know who I am."

RECRUIT FROM INSIDE THE ARENA

In 1910, Theodore Roosevelt delivered a famous speech titled "Citizenship in a Republic," best known for its "man in the arena" passage. Roosevelt wrote:

> It is not the critic who counts; not the man who points out how the strong man stumbles, or where the doer of deeds could have done them better. The credit belongs to the man who is actually in the arena, whose face is marred by dust and sweat and blood; who strives valiantly; who errs, who comes short again and again, because there is no effort without error and shortcoming; but who does actually strive to do the deeds; who knows great enthusiasms, the great devotions; who spends himself in a worthy cause; who at the best knows in the end the triumph of high achievement, and who at the worst, if he fails, at least fails while daring greatly, so that his place shall never be with those cold and timid souls who neither know victory nor defeat.

This powerful veneration of effort and perseverance—of living with skin in the game—has inspired people from Brené Brown, who titled her breakout book *Daring Greatly*, to LeBron James, who plays with the phrase "the man in the arena" inscribed on his shoes to remind himself to ignore critics and focus on his own effort.

Well-constructed support networks rely heavily on the people inside our arena, eschewing observers, critics, and bystanders for people who are shoulder to shoulder in the struggle. When Martha McCabe narrowed down her support network, the last group standing was the team that would be poolside with her. Similarly, if we return to a pair of stories that represent truly existential pressure—the cancer battles faced by my father and Sean St. John—both were marked by an almost sole reliance on support from within the arena.

While St. John never revealed his diagnosis to his colleagues at work and found his parents to be an added stressor rather than a support, fellow patients at the hospital were a huge source of strength and calm in the midst of his battle: "It's going to sound incredible, but I was more calm, more at ease, more confident sitting in the hospital than I was walking down the street to get a coffee. It was almost like a place to go to be surrounded with people that were dealing with the same stuff, and everybody was positive and energetic. We got this. It's going to be okay."

My father found that the greatest source of support through his ordeal, other than my mother, was talking to other people who had gone through their own battles with throat cancer. "I couldn't say 'You don't know what I'm going through' because they knew exactly what I was going through." Having been there before, these essential allies were able to prepare him for some of the tough realities of his treatment regimen—in his case, that things would actually get a lot worse for the two to three weeks after his radiation treatments ceased, a tough reality that he hadn't anticipated—while at the same time providing steady optimism that he would get through it because, heck, they did.

PROACTIVELY SET THE TERMS OF ENGAGEMENT

When I was six years old, I went to visit my half-siblings, who lived with their mother and stepfather in Calgary. Everything was going great until, after a wonderful dinner, I was offered ice cream for dessert. On seeing the carton pulled out of the freezer, I declined: "I'm sorry, we only eat Häagen-Dazs at our house." For the past 30 years, I have been reminded of this moment at every Easter, Thanksgiving, and Christmas without fail, both by my siblings—who experienced such visceral embarrassment on my behalf that the sensation has not left them decades later—and by my father, whose very good relationship with his ex-wife and her husband subsequently had to weather the storm of him being known as "Mr. Häagen-Dazs" for close to a decade.

When we are on the receiving end of support, it can feel presumptuous to do anything other than accept it gratefully. No one wants to be the snotty six-year-old kid who turns up their nose at a free dessert. And yet, the people who are best at leveraging support are also exceptional at proactively setting the terms of engagement for their support networks. Again, consider Martha McCabe's story, in which she laid down very clear guidelines for her family: when I'm at the Games, don't call me; I will call you. This wasn't done to be rude—it reflects the fact that if support is truly going to be supportive, it ultimately needs to serve the needs of the performer, not the emotional wake of the support system.

FINDING YOUR
TOP FIVE

Across all of my conversations, what I've learned is that the best way to be truly supported under pressure is through a small group of people who are:

- "in the arena" with you;
- not prone to the pity party;
- able to allow their emotional wake to take a back seat to your needs; and
- consistently focused on what you need to do, not what's at stake.

How many people in your life would you describe in those terms? To go back to what Jim Rohn said: "You are the average of the five people you spend the most time with." If your top five don't meet that description, you may not be getting the support you need.

Once you've found those people, if they're the right people, you'll be able to have an open and honest conversation around what support looks like—both for them and for you.

CHAPTER 11

——

PRESSURE, ATTENTION, AND PREPARATION

USING THE PRESSURE CANVAS

So how do you break through under pressure? As you've seen, the answer is: it depends. Sometimes it's about connecting with why it matters; other times it's about not becoming overwhelmed by importance. Sometimes it's about immediate, direct action; other times it's about accepting that you can't act. Sometimes it's about gathering all the support you can; other times it's about keeping your circle tight.

The one thing that is a constant, regardless of the specific tactics used to deal with pressure, is the need for preparation. Almost uniformly, people who are exceptional under pressure point to the importance of preparation. When Hayley Wickenheiser summed up what has underpinned her success, she said: "I really trust myself in knowing how to prepare. I think that was probably my greatest strength as an athlete—and I think it's what is serving me well in medicine too." When I spoke with Curt Cronin, he talked extensively about the highly disciplined mental preparation process that every navy SEAL goes through well before they are placed in a combat situation. In particular, he emphasized the value of knowing how to prepare, even if you don't know precisely what you're preparing for: "Because we knew how to prepare, we were confident that we could overcome anything that came our way. Now, sometimes that's perceived as 'Oh, you had prepared for everything.' No, no, no. We prepared for everything we possibly could, but every deployment required doing things I'd never seen before. But because we learned how to prepare together, in a variety of circumstances, we learned how to prepare for circumstances we never could have foreseen."

In many ways, if you're looking for a true antidote to pressure it's strikingly simple: preparation.

Gerry Butts, the former principal secretary to Canadian prime minister Justin Trudeau and the architect of two consecutive federal election victories for the Trudeau Liberals, summed this principle up succinctly as "plan beats no plan every time." Butts has lived a life of pressure: he was an athlete in high school, a two-time national debate champion during his time at McGill University, and the CEO of the World Wildlife Fund for four years, and has held senior positions in provincial and federal government for the better part of 20 years. When I asked him about the most pressure he's ever faced, he didn't hesitate. It was the two weeks between February 18, 2019, when he resigned his post as Trudeau's chief advisor, and March 6, 2019, when he delivered two hours of televised testimony on his role in the SNC-Lavalin affair to the House Judiciary Committee. "I hope to never again have to do two hours of live television on a major national political issue," he reflected when we spoke just over a year after that tumultuous period. With maple trees swaying gently in the background of Butts's Ottawa home, our conversation felt far removed from the pressure cooker of 15 months prior, but the detail with which he could recall those 16 days made it clear that it had left a lasting imprint.

Butts made the decision to resign two days before he announced it. Despite being sure that he had done nothing wrong, he had come to believe that, with the growing heat and light on both him and the prime minister around whether they had pressured the attorney general to intervene in a corruption case facing the engineering firm SNC-Lavalin, his resignation and subsequent testimony was the bitter medicine required to move past a situation that had the potential to bring down the government he had worked for years to build.

When he announced his resignation, it hit like a tidal wave. It was front-page news from coast to coast and, depending on the political leanings of the reporter, hailed as everything from the difficult decision of a principled man to a damning admission of guilt from Trudeau's inner circle. For Butts, the media's response was "10 times what I thought it was going to be. I had five TV cameras at the end of my driveway. I got hounded by the *Globe and Mail* while walking my kid to school." Butts was unprepared for the intensity of the media's insertion into his personal life. "I didn't have a plan. I knew why I was doing what I was doing, but . . . I had not yet developed a plan to deal with it. So that was probably the moment of maximum pressure." Butts went on: "One of the key constituent parts of pressure for me is a loss of control. You feel like you're in the midst of chaos where nothing you do will affect the outcome. And those are the most challenging situations. It's almost crushing."

Amidst the already emotional decision to resign, Butts felt completely thrown off balance, shocked by the magnitude of the reaction and livid at the media's intrusions into his family life. He was at the mercy of the pressure rather than in the driver's seat— not where you want to be with less than two weeks to prepare for a very public and high-profile performance.

"My wife sort of saved my life in that whole situation," Butts says. "I called it the Saigon airlift. She said, 'We're getting out of Ottawa and going to Toronto. We're going to surround ourselves with our closest and smartest friends, and we're going to sit down for a couple of days and think this through and talk about how we're going to deal with this situation.' That was essential." Butts closed ranks and, with the support of his wife and most trusted friends, did what he'd always done in the past: he prepared. He redirected his focus away from the myriad things he couldn't control and focused intensely on the process of getting ready to testify. How does one prepare to go on national TV and get grilled? It starts, of course, with building confidence in your material. Just as an elite figure skater needs to ensure they have overtrained their routine to the point that it's automatic, Butts needed to know his material cold, "to know precisely what you're going to say and why you're going to say it. And to be able to think through beforehand all the potential ways people could construct questions that can lead you down blind alleys." Working with his team, he started by hammering out the broad narrative and working down to the finest details. They called it the "funnel" approach.

Now, being prepared on substance is one thing; being prepared for the bright lights is another thing entirely. "In my life, I have never exhibited more physical symptoms of stress than I did that week in the lead-up [to testifying]," recalls Butts. In the immediate moments before leaving the waiting room to speak— with the nation's eyes on him both literally and figuratively—he leaned over to his wife. "I said, 'I don't know how I'm going to walk from the door to my seat without throwing up.' That's how I felt. I meant it literally. I've been in the situation many times where somebody else is speaking and I'm walking through a bank of cameras with them. But I'd never had those cameras trained on me."

With the cameras pointed squarely at him for the first time, he had a familiar ally: preparation. "One of the lawyers we were working with warned me that I was going to feel that way." As uncomfortable as the nausea, weak knees, and sweaty palms were, Butts knew to expect them and had a plan. His lawyer had worked with him specifically on this moment. "She said, 'The key thing is to just start talking and keep talking. For your first couple of paragraphs your mouth is going to be dry, you're going to feel like you're shaking, you're going to wonder whether you can get through this. You'll feel like everybody can see it, but nobody will notice anything. The key is, just keep talking.'" Which is exactly what he did. You can watch the tape—his lawyer was right.

"What was most helpful for me was having a playbook," Butts says. "It's always been what's most helpful for me. I've been that way since I was a little kid playing Little League. I would annoy the coach with 'How are we going to win this game? What's the plan?' Plan beats no plan every time."

Adults hate being at the bottom of learning curves in general. Some of the most uncomfortable situations we face come from being asked to do something we don't feel we're good at in a public environment. Under pressure, the discomfort of trying new things is hugely magnified. In Chapter 2, I noted that when we become activated our attentional focus narrows and we retreat to what we know best. We have a hard time accessing information, and our capacity for learning is greatly diminished. Effectively handling pressure isn't an improv exercise—it's not the time to try something out just to see what works. As Archilochus noted over 2,000 years ago, under pressure "we don't rise to the level of our expectations, we fall to the level of our training."

Practically speaking, if you hope to get any benefit from the skills and strategies outlined in this book when you are *actually* under pressure, it's not a good strategy to simply hope they are there when you need them. Breaking through under pressure requires preparation. So let's talk about how to take the ideas in the preceding pages and use them to create an effective mental preparation plan for handling pressure. First, we need to get reacquainted with all of the tools or tactics that might go into the plan, with a summary of the key tactics from each area of the pressure equation.

PEAK PRESSURE MOMENTS

In peak pressure moments, we become most acutely aware of our body's often suboptimal responses to extreme pressure. The sympathetic nervous system floods the body with adrenaline and cortisol, our heart rate and breathing accelerate, and our sensory gating goes into overdrive, narrowing our peripheral vision and, in extreme cases, our hearing. In Chapter 2 we learned about police officers who failed to hear shots fired or to see obvious landmarks when under extreme pressure. In Butts's case, the physical response went as far as nausea and shaking.

In this hyperactivated state, we need to get our physiology under control before we can move on to other strategies. Heather Watt, the chief of staff to the Ontario minister of health, faced crucial decisions in the early days of the COVID-19 crisis that would impact 14.5 million people, and realized that the only way to calm her racing mind was to breathe. Breathing is our first port of call in peak pressure moments. From there, we can move on to the strategies we learned from the pressure equation:

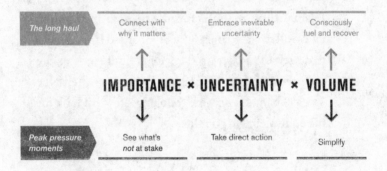

IMPORTANCE

The core goal in peak pressure moments is to ensure that we are seeing things in the appropriate perspective. Ten days before the Olympics, Johann Koss, crying under a stairwell, said he left like "failure [at the Olympics] would create failure for the rest of my life" until a conversation with his sport psychologist reminded him that, as important as it was, the Olympics wasn't a referendum on his life. In particular, his aspiration of becoming a medical doctor when he retired from skating wasn't at stake.

The key tactics we learned in this area were:

- **Seeing what's not at stake:** This is the discipline of rounding out your perspective so that you aren't solely focused on what's at play in a given situation but are also seeing what *won't* change, regardless of the outcome.
- **Working to deflate ego-driven stakes:** Andrew Blau called this the chase of "psychic validation"—when we layer on additional stakes that are about how we will be perceived or how we will perceive ourselves.
- **Dismantling manufactured urgency:** In the digital world, we are constantly bombarded by messages that seek to ratchet up the feeling of urgency or the importance of acting quickly. Remember the ONLY 3 LEFT! banners on hotel booking sites and look for the equivalents in your life.

UNCERTAINTY

When it comes to uncertainty, the main objective under peak pressure is to establish a beachhead of certainty by taking direct action on something we can control. When Curt Cronin unpacked his peak pressure moment on deployment, he recognized after the fact that calling in the helicopters might have been the second- or third-best option, but making a decision and taking action quickly was the best choice in the moment to stave off pressure and fear for his unit. Focusing on what we can control and beginning to make progress connects us with our capacity for self-efficacy and starts to alleviate the sense of helplessness that is at the root of the negative impact of stress. We saw this in spades in Gerry Butts's story earlier in this chapter.

The key tactics we learned in this area were:

- **Identifying your "serve"**: When beach volleyball player Martin Reader was preparing for the biggest match of his life, he isolated the one thing he had complete control over: the serve. Under peak pressure, identify your serve.

- **Building routines**: Brian Orser recognized that whether he would skate first, fourth, or sixth at the Olympics wasn't up to him, but he could build a routine for every possibility and create a sense of certainty and predictability that way. Routines are a great way to redirect focus from outcomes to behaviors.

- **Focusing on breathing**: Breathing is one of only two things in the body that happens automatically but can also be controlled consciously. When you focus deliberately on establishing a rhythm of 6 belly breaths per minute, you not only immediately impact our physiology, but also exert control and see progress.

- **Changing your perspective**: When all else is outside of our control, you can choose to see what you are learning in a difficult situation, why the situation matters to you, and how people you aspire to emulate would handle this adversity. In this way, you connect with what Victor Frankl calls "the last human freedom"—the ability to choose how we see what we are going through.

VOLUME

In the face of volume, we often turn to time management, but that's a trap. Time management is great for efficiency but not so great for alleviating pressure. When it comes to peak pressure moments, the key is to eliminate as much volume as we can. Distraction is the enemy, and even "positive pressure" is still added pressure. Swimmer Martha McCabe ditched her existing SIM card in the lead-up to the Olympic trials so she could control who had her number and therefore access to her time.

The key tactics we learned in this area were:

- **Separating foreground and background:** Building on Andy Higgins's training guidelines of "school, social life, athletics—choose two," if you can identify what areas of your life to place in the foreground and which to relegate to the background, you will gain clarity on what you are simplifying in service of.

- **Embracing structural simplification:** Get inspired by McCabe's cell phone story and create volume-free zones—like a blissfully Wi-Fi-free airline flight—to enforce simplification without relying on willpower.

- **Establishing absolutes:** Legendary Harvard professor Clay Christensen's maxim that it is "easier to stick to your principles 100% of the time than 98% of the time" led him to skip a National Championship basketball game. Identifying the absolute rules you will use to audit your volume can dramatically reduce the fatigue of triaging pressure and deciding what to say yes or no to.

THE LONG HAUL

Over the long haul, pressure tends to come less from overwhelming importance or acute uncertainty and more from the accumulation of huge volume amidst uncertainty. Whether it is carrying the weight of a pandemic response for over a year or carrying a grueling training load in service of winning a medal at the Olympics, when we operate under pressure for a significant period of time, it can feel draining. In addition, the narrowing of attention that occurs under peak pressure can start to become a permanent state, and we can lose sight of our lives outside of the situation that is creating the pressure.

Beyond exhaustion and tunnel vision, the long haul can have health implications. As Dr. Herbert Benson showed decades ago, long-term elevated adrenaline and cortisol levels are directly correlated to increased incidence of heart disease and cardiac events.

To avoid these traps and effectively navigate long hauls of pressure, we identified three main strategies linked to the pressure equation:

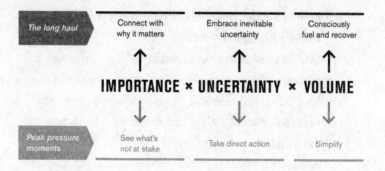

IMPORTANCE

The key goal for importance over the long haul is to keep it front and center. As Jeremiah Brown said: "At the end, what you are left with is the answer to the question 'Why are you doing this?'" Making it through the long haul without burning out requires a clear line of sight to why the pressure is worth it. Crucially, it isn't necessarily about finding "happiness" in the midst of the long haul; it's about finding meaning. And it's not all or nothing. The long haul will be fraught with ups and downs, with times when it is easier and times when it is harder to see meaning. Making it through the long haul is about savoring the moments of meaning—and ideally increasing the frequency with which they occur. Even my kids are a pain in the butt 80% of the time, but the moments we share in the other 20% make it all worthwhile.

The key tactics we learned in this area were:

- **Linking pressure to contribution:** A clear view of how carrying your load will benefit others is the primary tool for connecting with meaning. Rick Hansen was able to endure 26 months of physical and mental anguish across more than 24,000 miles because he had a clear view of how he was contributing to a world without barriers.
- **Linking pressure to growth:** When you connect with how pressure is strengthening you, you carry the load differently. Shaun Francis of Medcan contrasted his experience at a New York investment bank, where pressure was a cudgel, with the Naval Academy at Annapolis, where the pressure was intense but shaped to foster development.

- **Clearing a line of sight from your North Star to your daily decisions:** The real work under the long haul is fighting to ensure that you can see alignment all the way from meaning down through your vision and goals to your daily decisions. Jeff Dionne at St. Joseph's was able to clear a line of sight from fighting with a printer at 11 p.m. to produce an employee engagement survey all the way up to how the survey would benefit front-line workers, and his understanding of the meaning of his work ensured that his focus never wavered.

UNCERTAINTY

Over the long haul, managing pressure means accepting the limitations of control and learning to embrace uncertainty by simultaneously holding two seemingly contradictory beliefs: that the future is unknown and unknowable *and* that things will work out in the end.

The key tactics we learned in this area were:

- **Grooving in mindsets of dogged exploration:** Many high performers are trained to value mindsets of execution and efficiency, but as Melissa Quinn learned when integrating a design-led innovation firm into a strategy firm, these mindsets tend to be brittle in the face of uncertainty. Instead, we can learn from Bob Lurie's list of 40 ideas and his patient approach to crossing off the first 26 until number 27 finally fit the bill. With effort and practice, as Quinn has shown, you can groove in new mindsets that help you value uncertainty and exploration.

- **Playing Fortunately, Unfortunately:** Consciously reminding yourself that life is one long game of Fortunately, Unfortunately is a wonderful way to embrace uncertainty. When Christine Sinclair sat devastated on the field in the 2011 World Cup, she didn't know it yet but she was at the turning point that would lead to Canada's first-ever Olympic medal in soccer.

- **Expanding your view of victory:** An ability to never lose faith that you will prevail—to paraphrase Admiral Stockdale—is vital over the long haul. Often this means redefining what it means to "prevail" in order to see what you might learn, how you might be changed, and how the course of your life might be altered for the better in ways beyond your awareness in the moment.

VOLUME

Carrying volume over the long haul means focusing on how we acquire, conserve, and replenish energy. A strong foundation of sleep, nutrition, and movement forms the basis for our mental, emotional, and physical resilience over the long haul. As Phil Wilkins discovered when he suffered a seizure behind the wheel of his car in the midst of working 18-hour days for months at a time, there is only so long we can push through without taking care of ourselves.

The key tactics we learned here were:

- **Getting seven hours of sleep:** When you consistently get less than seven hours of sleep a night, not only does your cognitive performance resemble that of someone who is drunk, but you put yourself at risk of significant long-term health complications. Over the long haul, it is vital to embrace good sleep habits, like those outlined in Chapter 9.

- **Keeping blood sugar levels constant:** When Nicole Springle starts working with an athlete, blood sugar levels are her number one area of investigation. Keeping your blood sugar levels in a stable, predictable range is a great way to optimize energy and stave off fatigue. Work on this goal by eating low-GI foods at predictable intervals.

- **Making time for movement:** Exercise moderates how activated we get under pressure and stabilizes mood. A Harvard study showed that replacing 15 minutes of sitting with a 15-minute run had demonstrable effects on mood, as did replacing 60 minutes of sitting with a brisk 60-minute walk.

THE ONE SKILL TO RULE THEM ALL

So there you have it: 18 different clubs in the bag, 18 chef's knives in the set—whatever metaphor suits you best. You now have an array of tactics that you can deploy whenever you're navigating peak pressure or the long haul. Now, although it's great to have choice, 18 is a big number; it's a lot of tactics to incorporate into a preparation plan when you're heading into a high-pressure situation. Here is the good news: there aren't really 18 tactics. Ultimately, there is only one: attentional control.

You see, everything we've talked about in this book is underpinned by the fundamental human ability to consciously direct our attention. At Third Factor, we talk about our attention as a spotlight. Whatever we're turning our attention to is highlighted and, for the moment, everything else recedes into the background. When we talk about navigating peak pressure periods by focusing on what's not at stake, that's about directing the spotlight of our attention to the areas of our life that are not in play. When we talk about establishing certainty by focusing on routines, that's about directing the spotlight of our attention away from outcomes and toward behaviors. When we talk about connecting with meaning, that's about directing the spotlight of our attention away from our current pain or adversity and toward what we are contributing. And so on. The ultimate solution to the pressure equation is being able to consciously and deliberately direct the spotlight of our attention to focus on the thoughts, beliefs, and habits that support us rather than undermine us.

And so, when we are working to come up with a mental preparation plan, the goal is to establish where we will direct our attention for maximum benefit. In Gerry Butts's case, the plan was to direct his attention fully to the words on the page—to consciously *avoid* acknowledging his nauseous stomach, his shaky hands, and the crowd of camera-toting onlookers, and concentrate solely on the words coming out of his mouth.

Nothing has the power to focus our attention like a question. In the seminal book *The Inner Game of Tennis*, pioneering sport psychologist Timothy Gallwey showed a generation of tennis coaches that it is much more effective to ask questions *about* the ball than it is to continually yell "Watch the ball!" at people. When the coach asks "What brand of ball are you hitting?" the player has no choice but to watch the ball at a totally different level of intensity than they were previously. It's the question, not the command, that allows us to redirect our attention under pressure. Anyone who has ever repeatedly told themselves "Calm down!" knows that the command is rarely effective. This book is littered with questions that can serve as attentional anchors when you're under pressure:

- What's not at stake?
- How would I view others in this situation?
- What's my serve?
- What's the easiest thing I can do to make progress?
- What am I learning right now?
- What's the worst that could happen if I force action/ delay?
- How is carrying this pressure helping others?
- Will abandoning this lead to regret?
- What does "work out" really mean to me?

If you page through the book again with this lens in mind, you'll find these attentional cues everywhere.

THE PRESSURE CANVAS: A ONE-PAGE MENTAL PREP PLAN

Let's get really practical. If a mental preparation plan is ultimately about having cues to direct your attention, what does such a plan actually look like?

That's where the pressure canvas comes in (see Figure 8). It's a simple, one-page map that I've found invaluable in tying together the tactics discussed in this book. It offers a structured series of questions that give you attentional anchors you can use as pressure approaches.

While pressure can take many forms, this tool is predominantly meant to be used for a peak pressure moment that is preceded by a long haul period of preparation or anticipation. Practically speaking, many of our highest-pressure periods combine these two flavors: it is the template for everything from school exams to Olympic competition to big sales calls or presentations at work. To use the pressure canvas, you move across it, from left to right, as your peak pressure event approaches, using the questions as cues to tap into the strategies and tactics outlined in the book.

The example shown comes from a time when I was going to be onstage in front of 1,200 people for three hours and my performance would determine whether my firm would close our biggest sale of the year—a situation with a healthy combination of importance and uncertainty.

WHAT YOU NEED TO DO: *Deliver a speech in front of 1,200 people that will make or break our biggest sale this year.*

If peak pressure is preceded by a long haul of preparation:

Connect with IMPORTANCE	Prepare for ACTIVATION	Build CERTAINTY	Hold importance in PERSPECTIVE	Build a PLAN
What's at stake? - Finances - Cement an important new partnership	*How is your body going to feel under pressure?* - Increased HR - Jittery - Tense	*What is your average? What can you count on?* - No misses in 3 years – consistent delivery - Worst case scenario is that it is 'good'	*What's not at stake? What won't change regardless of the outcome?* - Love of partner + family - Tons of great friends - Successful business	*What 2–3 things will you say or do in the moment?* - Remind myself of my average - Hold what's not at stake in mind before taking the stage - Remind myself that activation is part of performance
Why does this matter to you? - Test of my ability to step up - Goal is to do many more big stage events	*How will you manage the discomfort?* - Recognize this is my body preparing me to perform - Diaphragm breathing - Humor	*What is your serve? What can you directly control in the moment?* - Deep diaphragmatic breath before taking stage - Opening 5 minutes – rehearse to death	*How is this helping you grow?* - If I can handle this, I can do any event	

AS PERFORMANCE APPROACHES

FIGURE 8: *The pressure canvas*

As you can see, I started on the far left by consciously connecting with why this event mattered to me and built motivation for putting in the work of preparation. This column is all about the "importance of importance" that we talked about in Chapter 4. In this instance, there was a fair bit at stake financially, and it would cement an important relationship. And it mattered to me personally, as it was one of the bigger stages I had been on at the time and I had set a goal to do more big stage events in the near future. In essence, it was a key milestone in my personal growth.

The canvas then moves on to physiology. As laid out in Chapter 2 and reinforced by Gerry Butts's story in this chapter, it is vital not to get thrown by the physical side of pressure. In advance, we want to get in touch with how we expect to feel and ensure that we have a plan in place to manage the discomfort. I felt a visceral weakness in my knees as I took the stage and, at one point, became worried that I wouldn't be able to hit the advance button on the slide clicker because of my shaking hands. Because I had strategies in place, however, I worked through it with some breathing, a joke I put in early in the presentation, and a clear thought of *This is what you expected—it's all good*. That's the value of preparation.

The third column is all about direct action and building certainty. Once the preparation is done, we want to remind ourselves of our baseline, or average. The question "What is your average?" comes from Brian Orser, and I've found it very helpful in reminding myself that, come what may, I can count on a certain level of performance. Then it's on to my serve—in this case, the first five minutes of the presentation, which was entirely within my control.

When your performance is imminent, it's on to column 4, which is all about keeping things in perspective and avoiding overwhelm. The key question "What's not at stake?" shows up here, as well as a reminder of how the pressure is helping you improve.

Finally, on the far right, we identify the two or three things we want to say, think, or do at the moment of performance to mitigate the pressure. This is where we take stock of the rest of the canvas and decide which of our attentional cues are the most helpful for us to carry into our performance. I'm happy to report that my speech went great and we closed the deal. Holding my three cues in mind helped me get over the hump of the first five minutes and settle into a rhythm.

I've included a blank canvas (see Figure 9), but, more helpfully, you can also download a PDF of it by going to danejensen.com /canvas. I've also provided a completely blank version, without any questions. That's because the questions here are just the ones that work well for me—you'll notice they don't encompass all of the tactics in the book. You may have your own favorite attentional cues, things I didn't put on here, like "How would I view others in this situation?" or "How are others benefiting because I'm carrying this pressure?" Ultimately, the specific questions that work for you will be personal. And I'd love to hear which ones resonate. If you create your own custom pressure canvas, please consider sending it my way, to dane.jensen@thirdfactor.com.

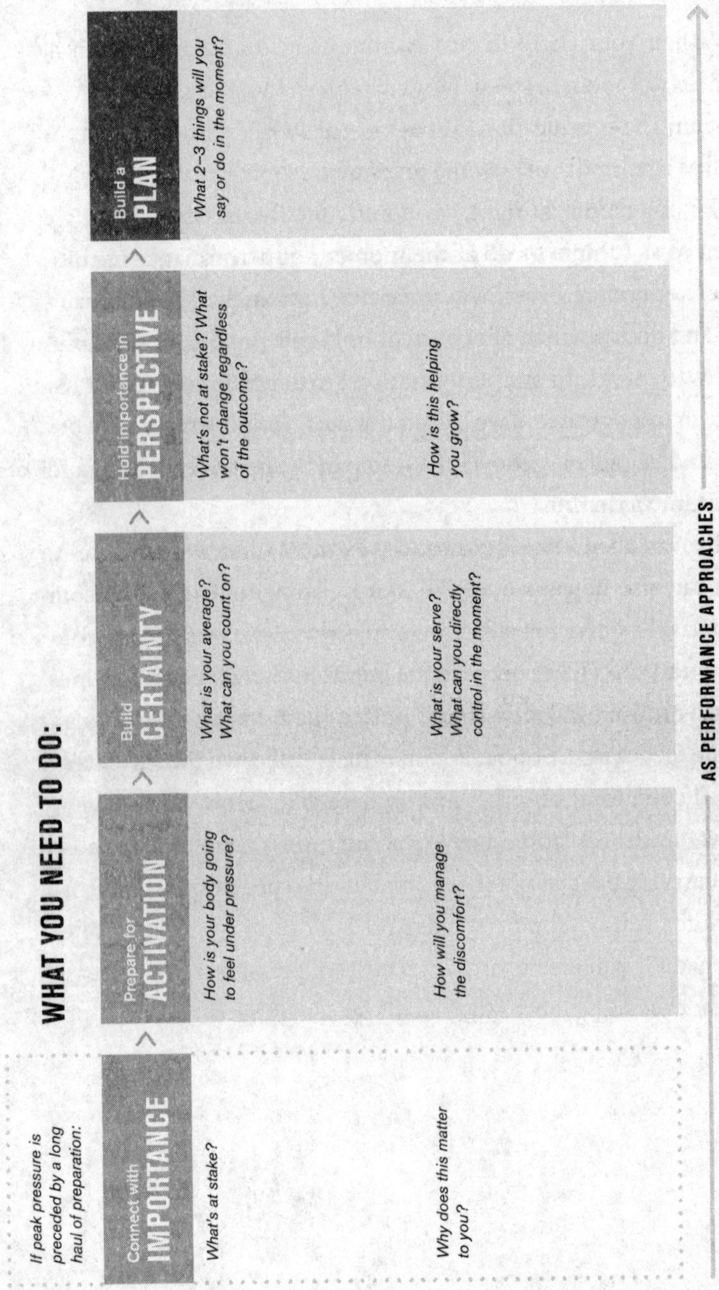

WHAT YOU NEED TO DO:

If peak pressure is preceded by a long haul of preparation:

Connect with IMPORTANCE	Prepare for ACTIVATION	Build CERTAINTY	Hold importance in PERSPECTIVE	Build a PLAN
What's at stake?	How is your body going to feel under pressure?	What is your average? What can you count on?	What's not at stake? What won't change regardless of the outcome?	What 2–3 things will you say or do in the moment?
Why does this matter to you?	How will you manage the discomfort?	What is your serve? What can you directly control in the moment?	How is this helping you grow?	

AS PERFORMANCE APPROACHES ──────▶

FIGURE 9: *The pressure canvas (blank)*

THE POWER OF
PRESSURE

Pressure gets a bad rap. In fact, a number of publishers I pitched this book to were much more interested in a book on being calm. Here's the simple truth: it's impossible for the vast majority of us to remain truly calm in the midst of highly important and uncertain situations. As we've seen, you can certainly be in *control*, but no matter how well trained you are, your body will activate. Your heart rate will rise and your breathing will quicken. Drawing on hundreds of thousands of years of programming, ancient systems will trigger an array of involuntary responses to put your body in a ready state and push your energy level up. But here's the good news: this energy surge can be way better than remaining calm. Pressure can give us superpowers if we know how use it. Pressure sets world records. Pressure fuels bravery. Pressure breeds persistence. Pressure is power.

So tap into it. As you tackle the important and uncertain situations that life will inevitably throw your way, use your spotlight to illuminate the hidden strengths that are waiting to be unlocked inside of you.

ACKNOWLEDGMENTS

Like every big project, this was a team effort. Chris Shulgan at Ghost Bureau (www.ghostbureau.com) helped me get it off the ground, and without his guidance, connections, writing, and editing, this project would be a shadow of what it is today. My agent, Chris Bucci, acted as a hybrid salesperson, hostage negotiator, and therapist to help me sell the book and navigate the world of publishing as a naive first-time author. My editor, Brad Wilson, believed in this book from the start, was a fantastic thought partner throughout, and provided a wealth of ideas for improvement. Book marketer extraordinaire Carolyn Monaco (www.monaco-associates.com) helped me understand how book sales really work, created a 200-row Excel spreadsheet for making this book a success, and acted as a combination of booster and taskmaster to bring it to reality. My publicist, Jill Totenberg (www.totenberggroup.com), pulled together what felt like an impossibly ambitious list of media partners and then made it happen. James Jensen and the team at Atom Studio took some chicken scratch and developed it into the wonderful diagrams and images you see here that enrich the text so much.

Many of the ideas in this book were formed, developed, and polished in conversation with the smartest group of people I know: the incredible training team at Third Factor. This book would have been a pamphlet without the wisdom of Peggy

Baumgartner, Cyndie Flett, Kara Stelfox, and Garry Watanabe—and a de facto member of the Third Factor training team, my incredible friend and colleague Melissa Quinn.

The broader Third Factor team all acted as editors, test readers, endorsement solicitors, and generally great partners. Thanks for all of your edits, notes, and ideas. Special thanks to Lori Quinn, Jordan Lavin, and Jon Fraser for leading the charge internally on the marketing and launch.

Of course, the lion's share of the content in this book came from interviews. I am forever grateful that so many busy, smart people took the time to share their stories. Whether it appeared directly in the book or not, every single conversation added a piece to the puzzle and enhanced the richness of the text. Thank you Andrew Blau, Dr. Andrew Petrosoniak, Anne Merklinger, Ben Cowan-Dewar, Bob Lurie, Brad Gerard, Brian Orser, Curt Cronin, Erin LeBlanc, Gerry Butts, Hayley Wickenheiser, Heather Watt, Heidi Tourond, Helen Naoumov, Jeff Dionne, Jenn Cruz, Jeremiah Brown, Jesse Goldhammer, Johann Koss, Karen O'Neill, Luc Mongeau, Dr. Marjorie Dixon, Martha McCabe, Melissa Quinn, Dr. Penny Werthner, Phil Wilkins, Rick Hansen, Rosie MacLennan, Sean St. Jean, Shaun Francis, Tracy Wilson, and others.

Without my parents there is no book. This is true both generally—I mean, I wouldn't exist without them—and also specifically. Without their work on pressure, performance, and life, the text could not possibly have been written. Our discussions over close to 40 years, but particularly in the last 10, have been the foundation for everything I know about pressure. This book rests squarely on the shoulders of their life's work of understanding what it means to be human, feel pressure, and perform.

And finally, to my wonderful wife, Hilary, who supported me in carving out space and time so I could write a book through a year-long global pandemic during which our three young children were underfoot most of the time. You carry the pressure of the long haul with such patience, grit, and kindness, and when the pressure gets to me, you are the rock that holds me to the ideals I've laid out here.

SOURCES

As I wrote in the introduction, this book originated from a deceptively simple question—"What's the most pressure you've ever been under?"—and emerged from hundreds of conversations. In particular, it is rooted in the wisdom and experience of the incredible people with whom I did more formal interviews, including: Curt Cronin, Dr. Penny Werthner, Heather Watt, Jeremiah Brown, Rick Hansen, Shaun Francis, Rosie MacLennan, Karen O'Neill, Ben Cowan-Dewar, Jeff Dionne, Johann Olav Koss, Andrew Blau, Dr. Hayley Wickenheiser, Dr. Andrew Petrosoniak, Martin Reader, Brian Orser, Tracy Wilson, Sean St. John, Jenn Cruz, Luc Mongeau, Melissa Quinn, Christine Sinclair, Dr. Marjorie Dixon, Martha McCabe, Phil Wilkins, Heidi Tourond, Anne Merklinger, and Gerry Butts. All of them added to the story tremendously.

CHAPTER 1

The journey to the pressure equation started in conversations with the founders of Third Factor (and my parents), Sandra Stark and Peter Jensen. Their work over decades as practitioners led them to a realization that the primary factors that push arousal level up are the importance of the stakes and the uncertainty of the outcome.

My work with both corporate and sport clients, in particular as COVID-19 emerged during the writing of the book, reinforced that for most people an additional dominant factor in pressure is volume.

Curt Cronin, whose story opens the chapter, is a deep thinker on all things pressure and performance, and our conversation helped me flesh out several ideas for the book, in particular on the nature of direct action and preparation. You can learn more about Cronin at www.leadingauthorities.com/speakers/curt-cronin.

CHAPTER 2

This chapter would not have been possible without two wide-ranging discussions with Dr. Penny Werthner, the dean of kinesiology at the University of Calgary, and ongoing conversations with my colleague Kara Stelfox. If you're interested in learning more about biofeedback and neurofeedback, which can be used to be understand and train your responses to pressure, I recommend starting at www.researchgate.net/publication/283327868_Managing_the_Stress_Response_The_Use_of_Biofeedback_and_Neurofeedback_with_Olympic_Athletes.

The research into attentional narrowing among law enforcement officers is from Alexis Artwohl, PhD, *Perceptual and Memory Distortions During Officer Involved Shootings* (AELE, 2008) and can be found here: www.aele.org/law/2008FPJUN/wb-19.pdf.

While our understanding of pressure and our physical responses to it has been greatly enhanced over the past couple of decades, if you are looking to get a foundational understanding of how the sympathetic and parasympathetic systems operate, it is hard to do better than the seminal work of Dr. Herbert Benson and his book *The Relaxation Response* (New York: Avon Books, 1976). It's short, practical, and straightforward. It's one of the books that I return to over and over again.

The work of Stanford professor and researcher Kelly McGonigal, who is a master of both her own research and of compellingly synthesizing and summarizing work from across the field, has continued to broaden our understanding of the variety of stress responses that can arise. A transcript of her TED talk, "How to Make Stress Your Friend," is available at: www.ted.com/talks/kelly_mcgonigal_how_to_make_stress_your_friend/transcript?language=en.

CHAPTER 3

Kyle Lowry's post-game interview on the definition of pressure originally aired in June 2019. You can find it in a variety of places online, including the Bleacher Report's YouTube channel here: www.youtube.com/watch?v=Jdx-7rBE0HY.

Jeremiah Brown and I have engaged in a dialogue on pressure that has extended over two years. To learn more about Brown's story, you can read his terrific book *The 4 Year Olympian: From First Stroke to Olympic Medallist* (Toronto: Dundurn, 2018).

CHAPTER 4

Kelly McGonigal's succinct summation of the relationship between meaning, pressure, and stress was a touchstone for me in thinking through the double-edged sword of importance. You can read more of her insights in her book *The Upside of Stress: Why Stress Is Good for You, and How to Get Good at It* (Toronto: Random House Canada, 2015).

Rick Hansen's Man in Motion World Tour is the definition of the long haul, and his autobiography, coauthored by Jim Taylor, *Rick Hansen: Man in Motion* (Toronto: Douglas & McIntyre, 2011) is a compelling view into what it takes to persevere in the face on ongoing pressure—and how to bring importance and meaning closer to our everyday lives.

The peak-end effect is a psychological heuristic that was first demonstrated in 1993 by the legendary researchers Daniel Kahneman, Barbara L. Fredrickson, Charles A. Schreiber, and Donald A. Redelmeier in a study titled "When More Pain Is Preferred to Less: Adding a Better End," published in *Psychological Science*, volume 4, issue 6 (November 1993), pages 401–405, available at www.jstor.org/stable/40062570?seq=1. The phenomenon was included in Chip and Dan Heath's book *The Power of Moments: Why Certain Experiences Have Extraordinary Impact* (New York: Simon & Schuster, 2017), which does a great job of synthesizing a variety of research on how we evaluate and remember experiences. The difference between our "in-the-moment" evaluations versus how we remember and evaluate experiences after the fact is central to how we make decisions over the long haul.

The model for drawing a line of sight from our North Star all the way down to our daily decisions is from my father's book *The*

Inside Edge: High Performance Through Mental Fitness (Toronto: Third Factor, 1991). This model is one that I have taught and used extensively for years, and it never fails to provide clarity.

When it comes to articulating what provides a sense of meaning and satisfaction over the long haul, Teresa Amabile and Steven Kramer's *The Progress Principle: Using Small Wins to Ignite Joy, Engagement, and Creativity at Work* (Brighton, MA: Harvard Business Review Press, 2011) is a thoroughly researched and compellingly written book on the primacy of progress as a source of engagement. It is a book I return to frequently, and it informed my thinking on the role of growth as a source of meaning over the long haul.

The importance of progress was reinforced in my discussion with Shaun Francis on the difference between a high-pressure environment focused on development and improvement (his experience at Annapolis) versus one focused on extraction (his experience in investment banking).

My discussions with Rosie MacLennan in 2020 and Jeff Dionne in 2019 were extremely helpful in rounding out the two additional sources of meaning—connection and contribution. While their circumstances may be extremely different, both are wonderful people who strive to imbue their daily decisions with a sense of meaning to navigate high-pressure lives.

CHAPTER 5

Beyond being an all-time Olympic great, Johann Koss has led a life full of positive pressure. After his Olympic success, he went to medical school to become a doctor. Following graduation, he founded Right To Play (www.righttoplay.com), a multinational nongovernmental organization whose play-based programs accelerate the development of over 1.7 million children every week. Following the Lillehammer Games, Koss worked with his sports psychologists Bente Marie Ihlen and Heidi Ihlen to coauthor *Effect: Exploring the Distance Between What You Said and What I Heard* (self-published: 2012), which includes a very interesting look at the inner conversations that can fuel the positive or negative impacts of pressure.

The Eisenhower Box, as the name suggests, traces its origins back to a quote from US President Dwight D. Eisenhower: "I have two kinds of problems, the urgent and the important. The urgent are not important, and the important are never urgent." Eisenhower included this quote in a speech at the Second Assembly of the World Council of Churches at Northwestern University, and attributed it to a "former college president" that he did not identify.

The stories about Andrew Blau and Hayley Wickenheiser were excerpted from discussions held in early 2019. Both greatly helped my understanding of the different ways in which we can gain perspective on what is truly at stake and what is not.

I briefly cite two books in this chapter that I encourage anyone interested in the topic of awareness to read: Anthony de Mello's *Awareness: Conversations with the Masters* (Lloydminster, AB: Image, 2011), which is a collection of talks given by de Mello at various retreats, and Ichiro Kishimi and Fumitake Koga's *The Courage To Be Disliked* (New York: Simon & Schuster, 2019), a parable written in the style of a Socratic dialogue that explores the teachings of Alfred Adler.

CHAPTER 6

The opening of this chapter cites a University College London study carried out by Archy de Berker that shows the impact of uncertainty on acute stress responses. The full study, "Computations of Uncertainty Mediate Acute Stress Responses in Humans," was published in *Nature Communications*, volume 7, article number 10996 (2016), and can be found here: www .nature.com/articles/ncomms10996.

I spoke with Dr. Andrew Petrosoniak in late 2019 in a conference room at Toronto's St. Michael's Hospital. Dr. Petrosoniak is a renowned expert in the application of design thinking principles and in situ simulation training to enhance performance under pressure. Beyond his research and speeches, he is the cofounder of Advanced Performance Healthcare Design, a consulting firm that helps health-care organizations improve their performance and outcomes in critical situations. You can learn more here: www.advancedperformance.ca.

There is no better introduction to stoicism than William B. Irvine's *A Guide to the Good Life: The Ancient Art of Stoic Joy* (London: Oxford University Press, 2008)—my copy is well dog-eared and I return to it regularly. If you want to go straight to the source material, you can pick up a copy of *Meditations* by Marcus Aurelius, but it's a lot harder to parse if you're just getting started.

The concept of self-efficacy is central to this chapter, and to the whole field of resilience, pressure, and stress. Researcher, psychologist, and Stanford professor Albert Bandura first articulated self-efficacy theory in his seminal paper "Self-efficacy: Toward a Unifying Theory of Behavioral Change," published in

Psychological Review, volume 84, issue 2 (1977), pages 191–215, https://doi.org/10.1037/0033-295X.84.2.191.

A wealth of interviews and conversations provided specific insights and ideas for direct action. In particular, my discussions with Martin Reader on the concept of "the serve," Brian Orser on routines, Tracy Wilson on breathing, and Sean St. John on perspective were instrumental in taking the theoretical concepts of self-efficacy and direct action and making them as practical as possible.

No discussion on perspective is complete without Viktor Frankl's *Man's Search for Meaning* (Boston: Beacon Press, 2006). First published in 1946, it is the seminal work on the power to connect with our self-efficacy even in the most horrific conditions.

CHAPTER 7

The insight into the similarity between how the brain processes both uncertainty and pain comes from Olivia Fox Cabane and Judah Pollack's *The Net and the Butterfly: The Art and Practice of Breakthrough Thinking* (Toronto: Portfolio, 2017).

This chapter benefited greatly from the vulnerable and open storytelling of Luc Mongeau and the wisdom of Melissa Quinn, whose thinking on the impact of mindset on behavior—and, in particular, two different approaches to problem-solving as it relates to uncertainty—was key.

The Stockdale paradox was one of many powerful concepts articulated by Jim Collins in *Good to Great: Why Some Companies Make the Leap . . . and Others Don't* (New York: Harper Business,

2001), based on his conversations with Admiral Jim Stockdale. Stockdale was a student of philosophy and a committed Stoic. You can read his own account of his ordeal and how he persevered in *Courage Under Fire: Testing Epictetus's Doctrines in a Laboratory of Human Behavior* (Washington: Hoover Press, 1993), a transcript of a speech Stockdale delivered at King's College, London.

I had the great fortune to teach alongside Maria Gonzalez at the Smith School of Business, and her book *Mindful Leadership: The 9 Ways to Self-Awareness, Transforming Yourself, and Inspiring Others* (New York: Jossey-Bass, 2012) is a succinct and wise introduction to mindfulness and its application for leaders.

Finally, Dr. Marjorie Dixon is the living embodiment of never losing faith in the ability prevail. Her story was a touchstone for this entire chapter. You can learn more about the work done by Dr. Dixon and her team at Anova Fertility here: https://anovafertility.com.

CHAPTER 8

Martha McCabe is a two-time Olympian and the founder of Head to Head, an organization that pairs Olympian mentors with youth sport programs at schools and clubs. She has a wealth of insight into pressure and performance, and has chosen to pass it on to the next generation. You can learn more at www.headtohead.ca.

Marie Kondo was a big touchstone for this chapter. If you are not familiar with her work, you can watch her series on Netflix or start with her original text: *The Life-Changing Magic of Tidying*

Up: The Japanese Art of Decluttering and Organizing (Berkeley: Ten Speed Press, 2014).

To fully understand the uphill battle we all face in tuning out distraction and simplifying, you can read the full text of Sean Parker's incredible November 9, 2017, *Axios* interview, "Sean Parker Unloads on Facebook: 'God Only Knows What It's Doing to Our Children's Brains,'" here: https://www.axios.com/sean-parker-unloads-on-facebook-2508036343.html.

And finally, a debt of gratitude to an intellectual giant and one of the most impactful books of our era. If you haven't read Clayton M. Christensen, James Allworth, and Karen Dillon's *How Will You Measure Your Life?* (New York: Harper Business, 2012), do yourself a favor and pick up a copy. It gets at the very heart of how to make choices that simplify, without sacrificing what matters most.

CHAPTER 9

SLEEP

The research on the importance of sleep when it comes to handling pressure continues to grow. The comparison between the cognitive performance of sleep-deprived individuals and those under the influence of alcohol was published by Drew Dawson and Kathryn J. Reid in "Fatigue, Alcohol and Performance Impairment," *Nature*, volume 388, issue 6639 (August 1997), page 235, available at www.researchgate.net/publication/13990100_Fatigue_alcohol_and_performance_impairment.

For more insight into the emerging understanding of how sleep functions as the brain's "wash cycle," check out "One More Reason to Get a Good Night's Sleep," a TED Talk by Dr. Jeff Iliff. The video and transcript can be found at: www.ted.com/talks /jeff_iliff_one_more_reason_to_get_a_good_night_s_sleep /transcript?language=en. If you're interested in going deeper, you can also read the underlying research: Lulu Xie, Hongyi Kang, Qiwu Xu, Michael J. Chen, Yonghong Liao, Meenakshisundaram Thiyagarajan, John O'Donnell, et al., "Sleep Drives Metabolite Clearance from the Adult Brain," *Science*, volume 342, issue 6156 (October 18, 2013), pages 373–77, available at www.ncbi.nlm .nih.gov/pubmed/24136970.

A number of resources are available to help you better understand the impact of sleep on anxiety and emotional reactivity, including:

Anwar, Yasmin. "Tired and Edgy? Sleep Deprivation Boosts Anticipatory Anxiety." *Berkeley News*, June 25, 2013. https://news .berkeley.edu/2013/06/25/anticipate-the-worst/.

Chuah, Lisa Y.M., Florin Dolcos, Annette K. Chen, Hui Zheng, Sarayu Parimal, and Michael W.L. Chee. "Sleep Deprivation and Interference by Emotional Distracters." *Sleep* 33, no. 10 (October 1, 2010): 1305–13. www.ncbi.nlm.nih.gov/pmc /articles/PMC2941416/#B26.

Yoo, Seung-Schik, Ninad Gujar, Peter Hu, Ferenc A. Jolesz, and Matthew P. Walker. "The Human Emotional Brain Without Sleep—A Prefrontal Amygdala Disconnect." *Correspondence* 17, no. 20 (October 23, 2007): 877–78. https://doi .org/10.1016/j.cub.2007.08.007.

NUTRITION

Without Nicole Springle, the section on nutrition would have been greatly diminished. Her deep understanding of both the science and the behavioral side of nutrition were invaluable, and her willingness to share her terrific ideas (and snack suggestions) is so deeply appreciated. You can learn more about the sport nutrition services offered by Nicole and the team at the Canadian Sport Institute Ontario here: https://csiontario.ca/notre-expertise/sport-nutrition.

You can find more information on the glycemic index, along with a searchable database of the GI of thousands of foods at www.glycemicindex.com/index.php.

MOVEMENT

In the same vein as research into sleep, research into the links between movement and all aspects of performance and health continues to pile up. This study involving firefighters provides a useful view into how exercise impacts reactivity in acutely stressful situations: Laurie C. Throne, John B. Bartholomew, Jill Craig, and Roger P. Farrar, "Stress Reactivity in Fire Fighters: An Exercise Intervention," *International Journal of Stress Management*, volume 7 (2000), pages 235–46, https://doi.org/10.1023/A:1009574428627.

The links between movement and anxiety and depression over the long haul have been established in a number of studies, notably:

Conn, Vicki S. "Depressive Symptom Outcomes of Physical Activity Interventions: Meta-analysis Findings." *Annals of Behavioral Medicine* 39, no. 2 (May 2010): 128–38. https://doi.org/10.1007/s12160-010-9172-x.

Stephens, Thomas. "Physical Activity and Mental Health in the United States and Canada: Evidence from Four Population Surveys." *Preventive Medicine* 17, no. 1 (January 1988): 35–47. https://doi.org/10.1016/0091-7435(88)90070-9.

Most practically, a study out of the Harvard T.H. Chan School of Public Health on the links between exercise and depression shows that you don't need to do extreme, high-intensity workouts to access the benefits of exercise. Walking or running instead of sitting has a meaningful effect. An article on the research, "More Evidence That Exercise Can Boost Mood," can be found here: www.health.harvard.edu/mind-and-mood/more-evidence-that -exercise-can-boost-mood.

While nutrition, sleep, and exercise are introduced as separate topics, they are, of course, all interconnected. If you want to go deeper into the links between sleep, nutrition, movement, and performance, I highly recommend Greg Wells's *The Ripple Effect: Sleep Better, Eat Better, Move Better, Think Better* (Toronto: Collins, 2017).

CHAPTER 10

Before starting my formal interview process, I greatly underestimated the nuances of the interrelationships between pressure and support. The conversations with Sean St. John, Heidi Tourond, and Anne Merklinger were all essential in helping me see the double-edged sword of support.

The immense value of a properly constructed support network is supported through a number of seminal pieces of research. For more information on the West Haven Homecoming Stress Scale, which demonstrated the linkages between social support of veterans and PTSD, see David Read Johnson, Hadar Lubin, Robert Rosenheck, Alan Fontana, Steven Sonthwick, and Dennis Charney, "The Impact of the Homecoming Reception on the Development of Posttraumatic Stress Disorder: The West Haven Homecoming Stress Scale (WHHSS)," *Journal of Traumatic Stress*, volume 10, issue 2 (April 1997), pages 259–77, available at https://onlinelibrary.wiley.com/doi/pdf/10.1002/jts.2490100207.

The Grant Study is one of the most famous, and longest-running, studies in the social sciences. There are numerous books and articles that dig into its findings from various perspectives. For this chapter, I relied predominantly on Joshua Wolf Shenk's article "What Makes Us Happy?" *The Atlantic* (June 2009). You can read it online at www.theatlantic.com/magazine/archive/2009/06/what-makes-us-happy/307439/.

To dig deeper into the health impacts of social support, you can review the National Institutes of Health research that concludes "the effect of social support on life expectancy appears to be as strong as the effects of obesity, cigarette smoking, hypertension, or level of activity" here: Fatih Ozbay, Douglas C. Johnson, Eleni Dimoulas, C.A. Morgan, Dennis Charney, and Steven Southwick, "Social Support and Resilience to Stress: From Neurobiology to Clinical Practice," *Psychiatry* (Edgmont), volume 4, issue 5 (May 2007), pages 35–40, www.ncbi.nlm.nih.gov/pmc/articles/PMC2921311/.

CHAPTER 11

The central story of this chapter comes from my discussion with Gerry Butts in 2020. His candor in telling the personal story around a highly public and sensitive time was greatly appreciated and provided a North Star for the through line of preparation.

It is fitting that the closing chapter references W. Timothy Gallwey's *The Inner Game of Tennis: The Classic Guide to the Mental Side of Peak Performance* (New York: Random House, 1997). First published in 1972, it is a groundbreaking way of thinking about performance under pressure.

This final chapter also draws heavily on conversations with many of my Third Factor colleagues who have thought deeply about the tools of attentional control, notably Peggy Baumgartner, our Chief Learning Officer, and Sandra Stark, our co-founder.

INDEX

A

ABC response, 58, 61–62
action
    direct, 10–11, 23, 60
    pressure and, 9–11, 23, 26
Adler, Alfred, 107
Afghanistan, 9–11
Alzheimer's disease, 189, 190
Amabile, Teresa, 78–79
amygdala, 190–91
Anova Fertility and Reproductive
    Health, 159–62
anxiety, 101–4, 191, 214
Apple Inc., 109
attachment, 158, 198
attentional control, 252–53
attentional tunneling, 37–41
awareness (of self), 62–63

B

Bailey, Chris, 170
Bandura, Albert, 123
basketball, 47–48
belief, 158–62
    in things working out, 144–45,
        146, 154, 155–56, 157
Benson, Herbert, 41–42, 201
Berker, Archy de, 115–16
Binstock, Josh, 124–25
biofeedback, 27, 28, 29–32, 34
Blau, Andrew, 104–6
blood sugar, 203–8
Booking.com, 107–8
Boston Consulting Group, 39–40
brain. *See also* nervous system
    activity in, 32–34, 129–30
    breathing and, 129–30

brain (*continued*)
  and gut, 34–37
  pressure and, 42
  sensory gating by, 37–41
  sleep and, 189–91
Brand, Stewart, 104
breathing
  and the brain, 129–30
  controlling, 128–31
  as coping mechanism, 36–37,
    136, 137, 243, 245
  pressure and, 29, 30–31
  as sleep aid, 200–201
Brooks, Alison, 13
Brown, Brené, 234
Brown, Jeremiah, 49–52, 53, 54–56,
    57, 67–68
Buddhism, 144, 158
business mindset, 150–51
Butts, Gerry, 238–41, 252

complacency, 158–62
connection, 69–71, 81–83
  with importance, 84–87, 88–91
  and meaning, 81–83, 87
  to meaning, 73–74, 75–76,
    83–87
contribution, 79–80, 87
control, 119–23. *See also* uncertainty
  attentional, 252–53
  of breathing, 128–31
  letting go of, 119–20, 163–64,
    197–98
  limits of, 163–64
  of perspective, 131–34
  refocusing on, 123–24, 155
COVID-19 pandemic, 35–36
Cowan-Dewar, Ben, 167
creativity, 40–41
Cronin, Curt, 9–11, 23, 238, 244
Cruz, Jenn, 134–37, 233

C

Cabane, Olivia Fox, 139
Cabot Cliffs/Links, 167
Canadian Paralympic Committee,
    17–19
Canadian Sport Institute Ontario,
    202–3
carbohydrates, 206–8
Christensen, Clayton, 179–80, 246
coherence (physiological), 30–31,
    129
Collins, Jim, 154–55
communication, 155

D

Dawson, Drew, 187–88
decisions, 83, 84
DeRozan, DeMar, 47–48
design thinking, 148–49
diabetes, 203, 208. *See also* blood
    sugar
diet, 202–12. *See also* blood sugar
Dionne, Jeff, 88–90, 248
Dixon, Marjorie, 159–62
Doblin, Jay, 148
Doblin Inc., 147, 148–49
Dunfee, Evan, 226

E

eating habits, 202–12
ego, 104–6
Eisenhower Box, 108–9
Elliott, Christine, 35
emotions, 20, 206, 214. *See also specific emotions*
 sleep and, 190–92
empathy, 40
Eno, Brian, 104
epilepsy, 184, 188
exercise, 212–14
Expedia, 107–8

F

Facebook, 178
faith. *See* belief
fatigue
 emotional responses to, 190–92
 health risks of, 184, 188–89
 and performance, 187–88
Ferriss, Tim, 180
fight-or-flight response, 42–43, 44–45
Fishbach, Ayelet, 17
food, 202–12
Fortunately, Unfortunately (game), 152–54, 250
Francis, Shaun, 76–77, 248
Frankl, Viktor, 133, 156

G

Gallwey, Timothy, 253
George, Bill, 69

Global Business Network, 104–5
glycemic index, 208
goals, 83, 84, 87, 172
Gonzalez, Maria, 158
Good to Great (Collins), 154–55
Google, 109
Grant Study (Harvard University), 230–31
growth, 76–79, 87
 and meaning, 76–79, 87
 peak moments and, 172–73
 simplification and, 172–74, 175–77
A Guide to the Good Life (Irvine), 119
gut (gastrointestinal system), 34–37

H

Hansen, Rick, 71–74, 75, 79, 85, 163–64, 248
happiness, 71–76
health
 fatigue and, 184, 188–89
 pressure and, 41–42
 sleep and, 188–90
heart disease, 41–42
heart rate, 29, 30, 31, 129
Heath, Chip and Dan, 74–75
helplessness, 123–24, 147
Higgins, Andy, 168
"How to Make Stress Your Friend" (McGonigal), 44–45
"How Will You Measure Your Life?" (Christensen), 179–80
100 challenge technique, 198–200
Hyperfocus (Bailey), 170

I

Iliff, Jeffrey, 189–90
imagery, 134
importance, 14–15, 59, 60
    connecting with, 84–87, 88–91
    ego and, 104–6
    evaluating, 98–111
    over long haul, 67–91, 248–49
    in peak moments, 93–113,
        243–44
    refocusing on, 98–101, 103–4
    as relative, 111–13
    urgency and, 107–11
information acquisition, 40
information overload, 21
The Inner Game of Tennis (Gallwey),
    253
innovation mindset, 150–51
The Inside Edge (P. Jensen), 83
Irvine, William B., 119

J

James, LeBron, 234
Jensen, Dane. *See also* Third Factor
    experiences of meaning, 69–70
    experiences of pressure, 1–3, 20,
        67–68, 196–97
    experiences of simplifying, 173,
        179, 180–81, 215–16
    research on pressure, 3–5, 12
Jensen, Dorothy, 156
Jensen, Peter, 80, 219–20, 234–35
Jobs, Steve, 120, 122, 180

K

Keiser, Mike, 167
Kelly, Kevin, 104
Kishimi, Ichiro, 107
Knausgaard, Karl Ove, 94
Koga, Fumitake, 107
Kondo, Marie, 170–71, 172
Koss, Johann Olav, 93–97, 98,
        153–54, 243
Kramer, Steven, 78–79

L

Leonard, Kawhi, 47–48
Loblaws Inc., 143
long haul. *See also* meaning
    dealing with, 247–51
    importance and, 67–91, 248–49
    nutrition and, 202–12
    vs. peak moments, 22–23, 57–61
    pressure and, 22–23, 41–42,
        52–53, 59–60
    sleep and, 187–200
    and uncertainty, 139–64,
        249–50
    volume and, 183–216, 250–51
Lowry, Kyle, 47–48
Lukka, Lauri, 108
Lurie, Bob, 149–50

M

MacLennan, Rosie, 81–83, 101
Man's Search for Meaning (Frankl), 133
Marcus Aurelius, 119

Market2Consumer, 149–50

Mars Inc., 140–42

McCabe, Martha, 167–68, 174, 178–79, 197–98, 232, 234, 246

McGonigal, Kelly, 44–45, 67–68

meaning, 68, 69–87
    connecting to, 73–74, 75–76, 83–87
    connection and, 81–83, 87
    contribution and, 79–80, 87
    finding, 76–83
    growth and, 76–79, 87
    happiness and, 71–76
    over long haul, 67–91
    map to, 84–87

Mello, Anthony de, 121

Merklinger, Anne, 224–27

Mindful Leadership (Gonzalez), 158

mindfulness, 195, 198–200. *See also* awareness

Mongeau, Luc, 139–45, 146

Monitor Group, 147–49

muscle tension, 29

N

Nedergaard, Maiken, 189–90

nervous system, 26–27, 34–35. *See also* brain

The Net and the Butterfly (Cabane and Pollack), 139

neurofeedback, 27, 28, 32–34

North Star, 84, 85–87

nutrition, 202–12

O

Olympic Games. *See also* Own the Podium
    1994 (Lillehammer), 93–97
    2010 (Vancouver), 111–12
    2012 (London), 54–55
    2016 (Rio), 82–83, 226–27

100 challenge technique, 198–200

optimism, 154, 155, 173–74

Orser, Brian, 126–27, 245

Own the Podium, 224–27

P

Paralympic Games, 17–18, 71

Parker, Sean, 178

peak-end effect, 75

peak moments, 22–23, 37–41, 56–57
    dealing with, 242–46
    and growth, 172–73
    importance and, 93–113, 243–44
    vs. long haul, 22–23, 57–61
    pressure in, 22–23, 37–41, 56–57
    and sleep, 195
    uncertainty in, 115–37, 244–45
    volume in, 165–81, 246

performance
    fatigue and, 187–88
    simplification and, 174, 175–77
    sleep and, 187–88

pessimism, 156, 173–74

Petrosoniak, Andrew, 116–18, 125–26

planning, 104, 254–58

police, 38

Pollack, Judah, 139

Pontefract, Dan, 69

Porter, Michael, 147

The Power of Moments (Heath and Heath), 74–75

predictability, 125–28

preparation
    importance of, 237–42
    plan for, 254–58

pressure. *See also* long haul; peak moments
    and action, 9–11, 23, 26
    benefits of, 259
    and breathing, 29, 30–31
    coping tools for, 59–61
    defining, 13–14
    and goals, 172
    health impacts of, 41–42
    physiological responses to, 20, 29–45
    situations of, 12, 13

pressure canvas, 254–58

pressure equation, 12, 22

problem solving, 149–51

The Progress Principle (Amabile and Kramer), 78–79

protein, 206–7

psychic validation, 106–7

purpose. *See* meaning

The Purpose Effect (Pontefract), 69

Q

Quinn, Melissa, 147–49, 150–51, 249

R

Reader, Martin, 124–25, 245

regret, 174–77

Reid, Kathryn, 187–88

The Relaxation Response (Benson), 41–42, 201

The Ripple Effect (Wells), 215

Rohn, Jim, 228

Roosevelt, Theodore, 233

routines, 125–28

rowing, 49–52, 54–56

S

St. John, Sean, 131–33, 228, 234

St. Joseph's Health Centre (Toronto), 88–90

scenario planning, 104

Schwartz, Peter, 104

screen time, 180–81. *See also* social media

Segal, Michelle (pseud.), 15–16, 20

seizures, 184, 188

self-awareness, 62–63

self-efficacy, 123–24, 129

sensory gating, 37–41

setbacks, 153–54

simplification, 61, 167–81
    absolute rules and, 180–81
    audit process for, 175–77
    choosing priorities in, 167–75

and growth, 172–74, 175–77
implementing, 177–81
and performance, 174, 175–77
Sinclair, Christine, 152–53, 227, 250
Sinek, Simon, 69
sleep, 187–200
and the brain, 189–91
breathing drill for, 200–201
and emotions, 190–92
and health, 188–90
100 challenge technique,
198–200
importance of, 184, 187–92
improving, 192–95
over long haul, 187–200
and performance, 187–88
snacks, 209–12
SNC-Lavalin affair, 238–41
social media, 168, 178–79
speed skating, 93–97
sport psychology, 27–28
Spracklen, Mike, 51–52, 55, 56
Springle, Nicole, 202–3, 204–12, 251
Start with Why (Sinek), 69
Stelfox, Kara, 29–32, 187
Stockdale, James, 154–55, 156–57, 250
stoicism, 119–20
stress, 13, 213–14
suffering, 158
support (social), 155, 220–36
commiseration as, 223–24
importance of, 230–32
networks for, 232–36
as pressure source, 225–29
useful sources of, 224

T

Taylor, Jim, 73
temperature (body), 29, 31–32
Third Factor, 169, 195–96, 252. *See
also* Jensen, Dane
time management, 166, 171, 246
Toronto Raptors, 47–48
Tourond, Heidi, 222–24, 229
trigger responses, 61–63
True North (George), 69
tunnel vision, 37–41

U

uncertainty, 15–17, 21, 59–60. *See
also* control
accepting, 85–86, 118, 197–98
dealing with, 144–45, 146,
154, 155–56, 157, 159–62,
244–45
over long haul, 139–64,
249–50
paradox of, 145–46, 163
in peak moments, 115–37,
244–45
routines and, 125–28
The Upside of Stress (McGonigal),
67–68
Urban, Tim, 32–33
urgency, 107–11
US Naval Academy (Annapolis),
76–77
US Navy SEALs, 9–11, 238

V

Vaillant, George, 231
vision, 84, 85, 87
volume, 17–19, 21, 60, 61. *See also*
          simplification
     and long haul, 183–216, 250–51
     in peak moments, 165–81, 246
     of support networks, 232–33

W

Watt, Heather, 35–36, 243
Wells, Greg, 194–95, 215
Werthner, Penny, 27–28, 29, 33–34
Weston, Galen, Jr., 143
Weston Foods, 142–44, 145
White, Doug, 49–50
Wickenheiser, Hayley, 111–13,
          237–38
Wilkins, Phil, 183–86, 195, 250
Wilson, Tracy, 128–29
work life, 78–79, 184–86

Z

Zuckerberg, Randi, 168–69

Bring Dane Jensen
TO YOUR NEXT EVENT

- CONTRIBUTOR TO *HARVARD BUSINESS REVIEW*

- AUTHOR OF *THE POWER OF PRESSURE*

- ADDRESSED AUDIENCES IN 23 COUNTRIES ON 5 CONTINENTS

Through fresh stories and research, Dane shares how to sidestep the patterns that work against you—and harness the energy under pressure.

Your audience will learn how to:

- Apply the pressure equation to their benefit

- Recognize patterns under pressure that help and hinder performance

- Use new tools to meet their peak pressure moments head-on

To bring Dane to your event, email speaking@danejensen.com

Harness **The Power of Pressure**
IN YOUR ORGANIZATION

Bring the skills of *The Power of Pressure* to life through a virtual or in-person workshop from Third Factor.

Participants will learn how to:

- Consistently perform to their potential in their highest-pressure moments

- Stay committed and engaged through pressure over the long haul

- Use the pressure canvas to anticipate and plan for high-pressure events

- Understand the traps that accompany pressure, and how to side-step them

To get started, go to thirdfactor.com
or email us at mail@thirdfactor.com

GO BEYOND
The Power of Pressure

Dane Jensen's firm, Third Factor, has helped more than 30,000 people perform, collaborate , and lead more effectively in our disruptive world.

Offerings include programs in three key practices:

RESILIENCE · Learn how to perform under pressure and recover from setbacks.

COACHING · Learn the skills and tools world-class coaches use to produce results and build commitment.

COLLABORATION · Become a masterful collaborator—within and across teams.

Third Factor's faculty and programs are a driving force in influencing our culture. When I think of high performance, I think of Third Factor."

—*Ryan Garrah, president, Emerson Canada*

Explore the possibilities at thirdfactor.com
or email us at mail@thirdfactor.com